Management For Entrepreneurs

The Four Pillars of Management Every Entrepreneur Should Know

Dr. Noor Idlibi

Copyright © 2020 Noor Idlibi

All rights reserved.

ISBN: 978-1-953525-00-0

DEDICATION

To my lovely supportive wife Rollan.
and my sons Amr and Makeen, who are the inspiration of my life.

To my family, my lovely mother Seemon, and father Munir Idilbi who inspired me to follow his steps to become an author like him.

To every entrepreneur strives for success.

ABOUT THIS BOOK

You will learn the four pillars of management: planning, organizing, directing, and controlling, and learn how to apply them to turn wishes, dreams, and ideas into reality. You will become a better manager and leader.

You will learn how to create strategic and operational plans and put them into action to achieve your goals.

You will learn a lot of terms and techniques, such as Strategic Business Model, Line of Business LOB, Strategic Business Unit SBU, and Key Performance Indicators KPI.

You will be able to set SMART goals, do a SWOT analysis, and Gap analysis.

You will learn the organizing process and how to prioritize and group activities, and the most important techniques in time management to become more efficient and achieve the optimal results.

You will learn the directing process, effective communication, motivation. and its theories, and leadership, to become a great leader.

You will learn how to do the controlling process to make sure everything is going according to your plan, and how to do the right adjustment in case you have any deviation in the process.

Every entrepreneur needs to have this knowledge and acquire these skills to be a successful businessman.

CONTENTS

	Dedication	i
	Introduction	Pg 1
A	**Module One: Planning**	Pg 8
1	Chapter 1: Introduction to Planning	Pg 9

- Introduction to Planning:
- The concept of strategic planning.

2	Chapter 2: Strategic planning	Pg 14

- **Strategic planning steps:**
- **Planning to plan.**
- **Scanning the values.**
- **The Vision.**
- **The Mission.**
- Strategic business model
- Line of business. (LOB).
- Strategic business unit. (SBU).
- Key performance indicators (KPI).
- Strategic thrust.
- Organizational culture.
- **Performance audit.**
- **Gap analysis.**

3	Chapter 3: Operational planning	Pg 53

- **Integrating action Plan.**
- Setting SMART Goals.
- The Goal Table.
- **Operational planning**
- Conduct a SWOT analysis.
- Form SMART Goals from the SWOT analysis.
- Creating the goal table.
- The Time Table.
- The Task Table.
- **Coordination of integrated action/operational plan**
- **Contingency Planning.**
- **Plan implementation.**

| B | **Module Two: Organizing** | Pg 78 |

| 4 | Chapter 4: Introduction to Organizing | Pg 79 |

| 5 | Chapter 5: The Process of Organizing | Pg 82 |

- The Process of Organizing.
- Identification of activities.
- Grouping of activities.
- Assigning responsibilities.
- Granting authority.
- Establishing a relationship.

| 6 | Chapter 6: Organizing Grouping | Pg 87 |

- The Functional Approach.
- The Geographical Approach.
- The Production Line Approach.
- The Customer Approach.

| 7 | Chapter 7: Organizing principles | Pg 90 |

- Principle of specialization.
- Principle of functional definition.
- Principles of supervision or span of control.
- Principle of scalar chain.
- Principle of unity of command.

| 8 | Chapter 8: Time management. | Pg 95 |

- Benefits of time management.
- To Do List.
- Scheduling.
- Prioritizing.
- Task Analysis

| C | **Module Three: Directing** | Pg 104 |

| 9 | Chapter 9: Introduction to Directing. | Pg 105 |

| 10 | Chapter 10: Effective communications | Pg 108 |

- What is communication?
- Elements of communication.
- Encoder.
- Decoder.
- Message.
- Communication channel.
- Communication barriers.

- Basics of communication.

11   Chapter 11: Motivation   Pg 120

- What is Motivation?
- Motivation theories.
- Maslow's Needs Hierarchy Theory.
- Frederick Herzberg's Motivator-Hygiene (Two-Factor) Theory
- Douglas McGregor's Participation Theory.
- David McClelland's Need Theory.
- Job Characteristics Theory

12   Chapter 12: Leadership   Pg 137

- The definition of leadership.
- The definition of a leader.
- The definition of a follower.
- The characteristics of an effective leader.
- Skills that leaders should develop.
- The responsibilities of the leader.
- Differences between managers and leaders.
- Leadership styles.
- Types of Followers.

D   **Module Four: Controlling**   Pg 148

13   Chapter 13: Introduction to Controlling.   Pg 149

- Steps of the controlling function

14   Chapter 14: Setting Performance Standards.   Pg 152

- Kye Performance Indicators

15   Chapter 15: Measuring performance and types of Controls   Pg 156

- **Computerized Control Systems.**
- **Quantitative Measures of Control**.
- Gantt Charts
- Program Evaluation and Review Technique (PERT).
- Critical Path Method (CPM)
- **Customer Service Quality Control.**
- **Financial Control Measures.**

16   Chapter 16: Adjusting   Pg 195

- Comparing actual performance with standards or goals.
- Analyzing deviations.
- Taking corrective action.

INTRODUCTION

What is Management:

Scholars of management have defined management as the following:

According to **George R. Terry**, *"Management Is a distinct process consisting of planning, organising, actuating and controlling; utilising in each both science and art, and followed in order to accomplish pre-determined objectives."*

George R Terry (1877 - 1955).

Frederick Winslow Taylor, *"Management is the art of knowing what you want to do and then seeing that they do it in the best and the cheapest way."*

Frederick Winslow Taylor (1856 –1915).

Henri Fayol *"to manage is to forecast and to plan, to organise, to command, to co-ordinate and to control."*

Henri Fayol (1841-1925).

Harold Koontz, *"Management is the art of getting things done through others and with formally organised groups."*

Harold Koontz (1909-1984)

Peter Drucker *" Management is a multipurpose organ that manage a business and manages Managers and manages Workers and work. "*

Peter Ferdinand Drucker (1909 –2005)

And according to the **American Management Association**. *"It is the act of getting things done through others and having them do it willingly".*

We can consider management as the brain and the organization is the body, which cannot move or survive without the brain.

This brain is responsible for all movements of the body the good and the bad ones, it can protect that body or take it to its end. This brain can have a healthy body or it can have a sick body where it is just a matter of time before the death of that body.

As an entrepreneur, you are responsible for your organization, and you are the brain of that organization, if your management is poor, you are making that body (your organization) sick, and you are leading it to its end.

Without good management you cannot:

- Achieve your organization goals.
- Get the best utilization of resources.
- Increase the efficiency of your organization.

- Create a dynamic and good environment.

- Reduce cost and increase profit.

- Provide a sense of focus and direction.

- Maintain responsibility and order within your organization.

- Reduce workload.

- Create a good communication system.

- Monitor progress and develop your business.

- Motivate and create leaders who have are self-initiative.

- Hire the right people and reduce turnover.

And so much more.

Now we have seen how important management is let's have a glance over this combination of science and art which we call management.

Management in a glance.

We can divide management into four main areas:

1. Management Process
2. Functional Areas
3. Skills
4. Trends

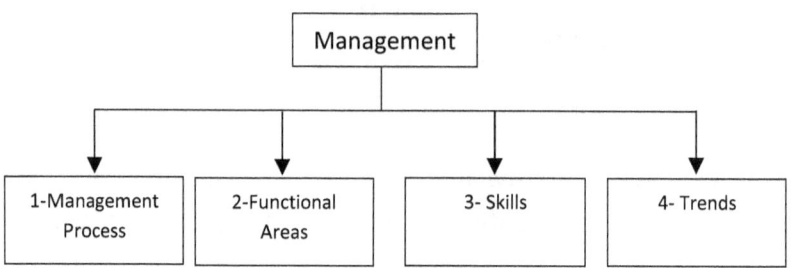

Management Process

Every successful entrepreneur and manager should learn the Management Process. It is a must to be able to practice management, without the Management Process you can't manage any kind of business or people properly.

Keep in mind you have to learn the Management Process to be a successful entrepreneur, and every manager or head of a department in your organization should Know the Management Process as long as he or she has employees to manage.

Management Process consists of Four Functions as follows:

- Planning.
- Organizing.
- Directing.
- Controlling.

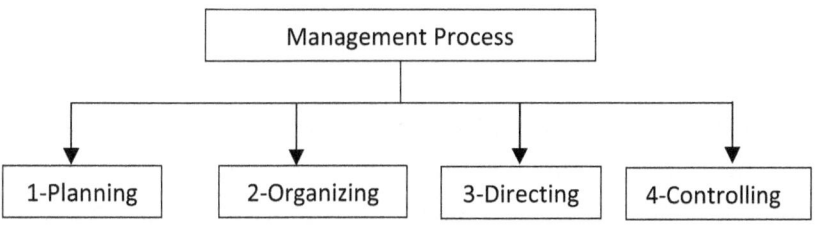

We are going to discuss each one of these Functions in detail further in this book.

Management Functional Areas:

Keep in mind that the Management Functional Areas are not a necessity for every entrepreneur or manager to learn, but it is a necessity to exist within the organization itself. So, it is a need for every organization but not for every entrepreneur or manager.

We can divide management functional areas into 6 main areas as follows:

- Personnel.
- Procurement.
- Finance.
- Production.
- Service.
- Marketing.

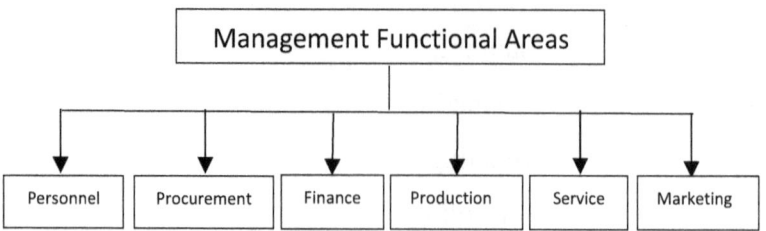

Skills

Skills are very important for every entrepreneur and manager, as much skills an entrepreneur or a manager can acquire as better performance he or she can give. Skills always come from practicing and experiences.

The most important skills that every entrepreneur and manager should work on are:

- Decision making
- Negotiation
- Meetings
- Presentation skills
- Active listening
- Delegation

Trends

It is always good to know the trends and keep up to date with what is going on within your industry, the benefit of that is to always be ready for any changes and be able to adopt.

The following are some example of management trends:

☐ Organizational behavior.

- ☐ Work team.

- ☐ Changing of (personnel and organizations)

- ☐ Learning organization

- ☐ Moralities.

- ☐ Online business.

In this book, we are going to focus on the four pillars of management which are:

- Planning.
- Organizing.
- Directing.
- Controlling.

So, let's start with the planning function of the management process.

MODULE -1-

PLANNING

Chapter 1: Introduction to Planning

Chapter 2: Strategic planning

Chapter 3: Operational planning

CHAPTER 1

INTRODUCTION TO PLANNING

INTRODUCTION TO PLANNING

Failing to plan is planning to fail.

Imagine the plan of an organization as a compass that leads the organization to the desired destination.

The importance of planning:

- Provides directions
- Helps in decision making
- Reduce risk
- Creates standards for controlling
- Reduces worthless activities
- Provides efficient utilization of resources
- Drives organizations towards their desired future status

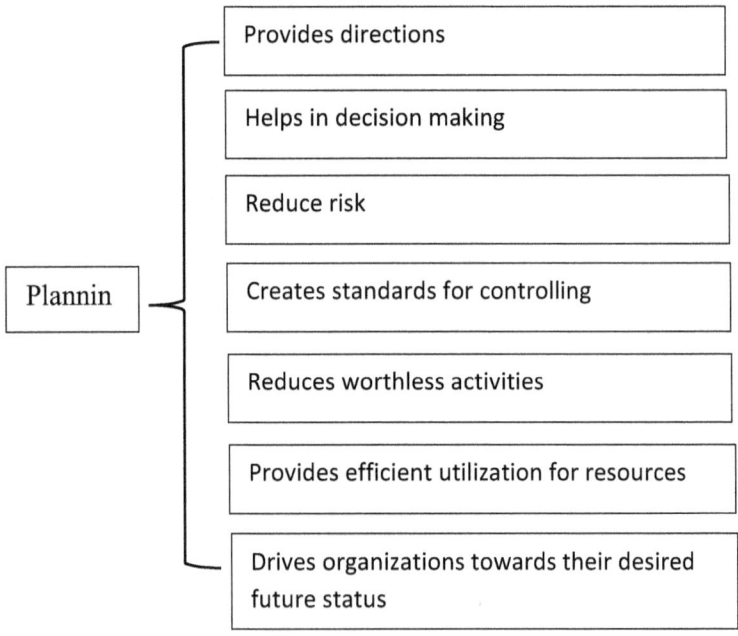

In planning, we have two main types that we are going to discuss in this book and these types are:

- Strategic planning
- Operational planning

In this book, we are going to discuss strategic planning and operational planning since they are the most common and popular planning types for organizations and as an entrepreneur manager, strategic and operational planning are the most important planning types you need to know.

That being said, let's get started.

What is planning?

Planning simply is a process of decision making to identify the direction of the future.

In other words, planning is to identify the following three things:

1- Where are we now?	(Our current situation).
2- Where do we want to be?	(Our desired situation in the future).
3- And how can we get there?	(The best practice that will lead us to get to the desired situation in the future).

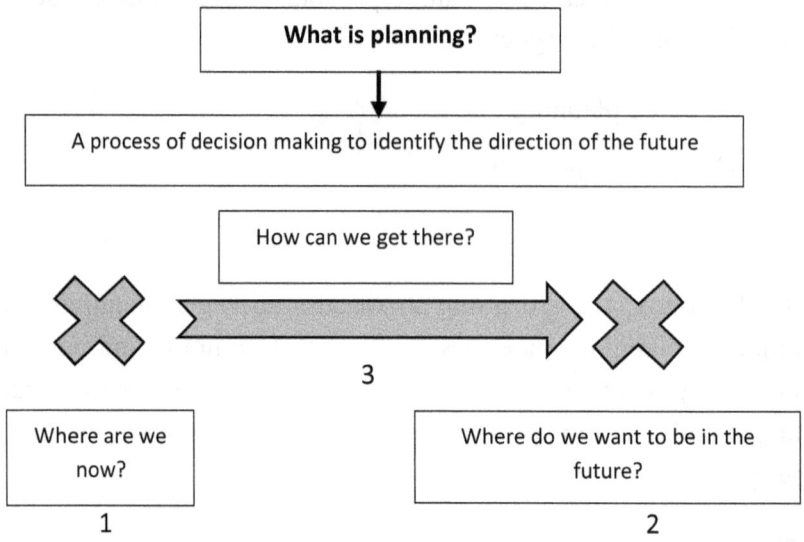

So, as we can see in the diagram above we need to identify our current situation or status NOW (Where are we now?) and then we need to identify our desired situation in the future (Where do we want to be?), but (How can we get there?) there might be a lot of routes to get to our desired situation, and here is the role of planning comes to play to choose the best path to get to our target by choosing the fastest, easiest, and less expensive path to get there.

Where we are now, that means to analyze our current situation or in other words, it is the **SWOT analysis** of our organization's current situation.

When we talk about where we want our organization to be in the future, that's what we call the **Vision** of the organization.

How can we get there? is our **Plan**.

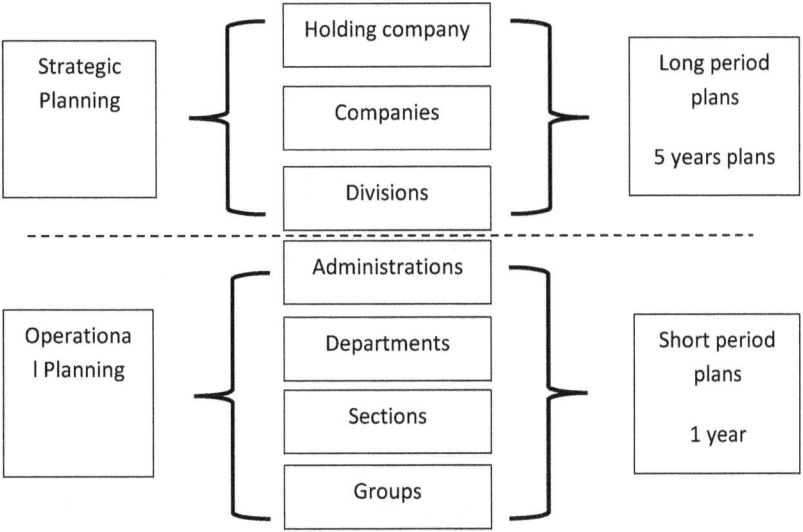

In the diagram above, you can see that strategic planning is for divisions and above, so we use strategic planning starting from divisions in the organization and going up because something as big as a division needs a long period plan, which is at least 5 years plan, and this is where we use strategic planning.

For smaller than that like administration or department or smaller, we use short period plans. So, operational planning is the right type of planning for this size of organization devices. Usually, operational plans come in a period of time of 1 year.

So, let's start with strategic planning.

CHAPTER 2

STRATEGIC PLANNING

STRATEGIC PLANNING

As a start let's ask this question, **what is a strategy?**

A strategy is a set of actions designed to achieve a major overall goal.

So, you can consider the path to take you from your current situation through certain types of actions to your desired future situation as a strategy.

The concept of strategic planning

Strategic planning is a process of determining a vision for the desired future status for an organization, as well as identifying its goals and objectives, and allocating the available resources to plan the process to reach its stated vision.

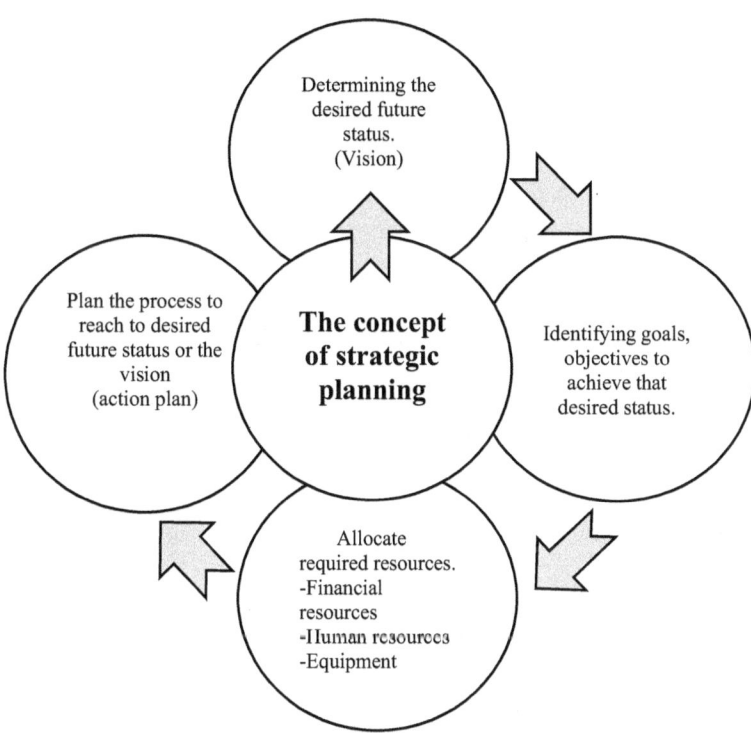

There are many types of strategic planning but we are going to focus on one of the most effective ways for entrepreneurs and businesses which is Pfeiffer strategic planning.

In strategic planning, we are preparing a plan for a long period of time starting from 5 years, and it goes up to 20 years depending on the size of the company or the organization.

Pfeiffer is one of the management scholars, he has his famous book **applied strategic planning** which is one of the best strategic planning models. This is why I chose to rely on this model to simplify strategic planning in this book

Strategic planning steps:

1- Planning to plan.
2- Scanning the values.
3- The Vision.
4- The Mission.
5- Strategic business model.
   - A- line of business. (**LOB**)
   - B- Strategic business unit. (**SBU**)
   - C- Key performance indicators. (**KPI**s)
   - D- Strategic thrust.
   - E- Organizational culture.
6- Performance audit.
7- Gap analysis.
8- Integrating action Plan/The creation of the operational plan.
9- Coordination of integrated action / operational plan.
10- Contingency planning.
11- Plan implementation.

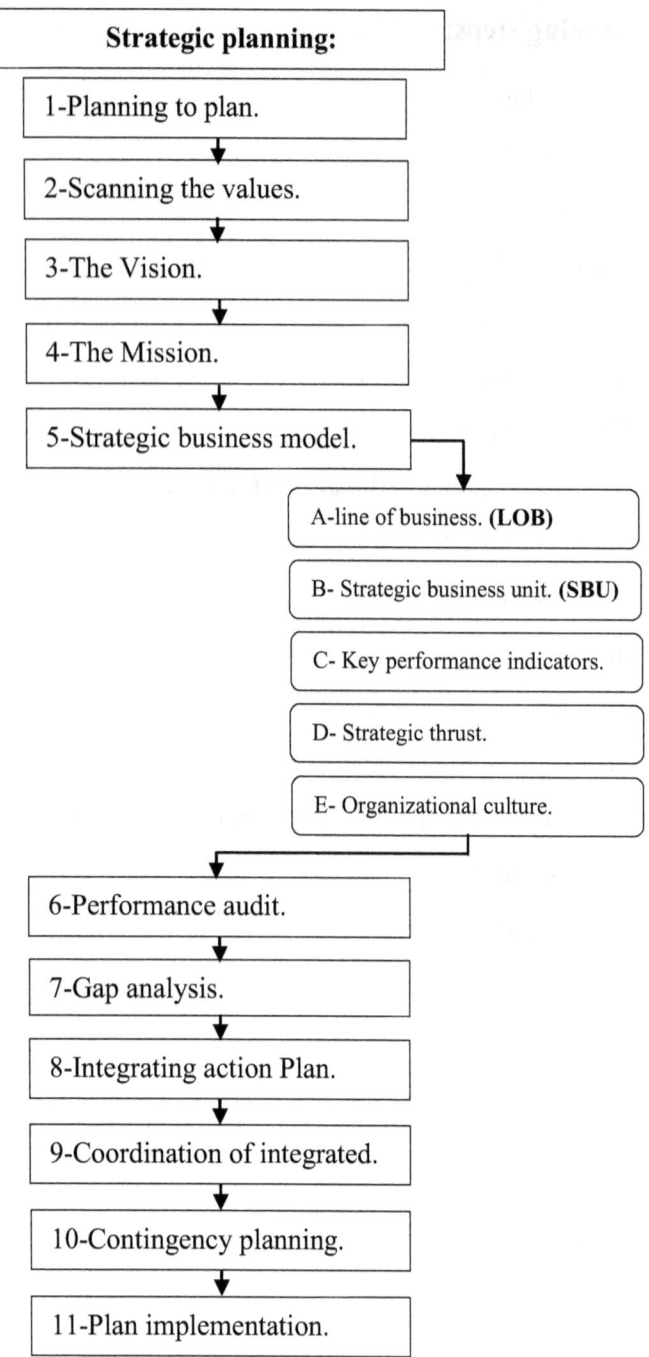

The first step in strategic planning is:

1- Planning to plan - Step 1

In this step we need to perform a few steps as follows:

A. *Forming the planning team.*

To form the planning team, we need to do the following:

The number of individuals in the team should be from 5 to 7 persons.

Why it should be from 5 to 7 persons? simply because if we have less than 5 persons in the planning team, we will have a lack of information, and more than 7 individuals, things like discussions and taking decisions are going to be difficult, complicated, and it will take more time.

There is also another reason why the number varies from 5 to 7, and that's because we can have one person who is an expert in two majors or we might have more than one person working together in the same field of expertise as you will see below.

Who are those people who will form our planning team, and what are their qualities?

There should be one who is an expert in the essence of the work of the organization.

For example; if the company major work is a real estate business, one of the team should be an expert in real estate, and we also need an expert in the competitors in the market, an expert in finance, an expert in human resources, an expert in Information technology, an expert in marketing, and the head of the team who is an expert in strategic planning.

In summary, the team should be like the following

1. An expert in the essence of the business.
2. An expert in the competitors in the market.
3. An expert in finance.
4. An expert in human resources.
5. An expert in IT.
6. An expert in marketing.
7. An expert in strategic planning and he is the head of the team.

Note:

In case we don't have an expert in one or more of these fields of expertise, we should hire or outsource consultants who are experts in what we lack, to form our planning team.

B. Deciding the period of writing the plan (How long it will take the team to finish the plan?).

Writing the plan should not take more than 6 months, no matter how big is the organization.

C. Deciding the period of the plan (how long is the plan itself?).

The answer is

- Small organizations (less than 100 employees) plan for 5 years.
- Medium organizations (100 to 500 employees) plan for 10 years.
- Large organizations (more than 500 employees) plan for 15 to 20 years.

D. Deciding on a system to manage the planning team.

That should discuss the following:

- When to meet.
- Where to meet.
- The system of exchanging information. (what kind of authorities the team has).

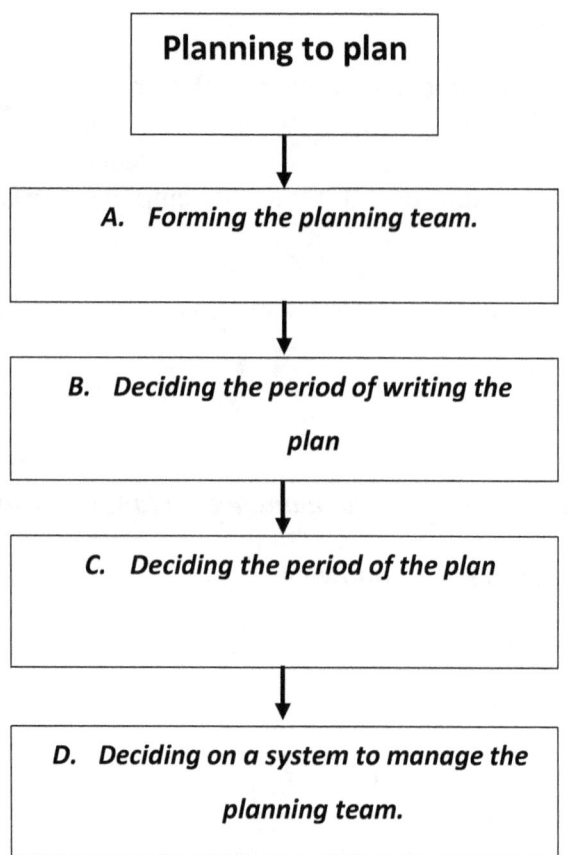

2- Scanning the Values - Step 2

This is the second step in strategic planning, in this step we need to identify the values that we want to adopt to create the culture of the organization.

An organization's core values are what support the vision, shape the culture, and reflect what the organization's values are to the outside world. They are the essence of the organization's identity, principles, beliefs, and philosophy of the organization.

Establishing strong values provides both internal and external advantages to the organization:

- Core values help organizations in the decision-making processes. For example, if one of your core values is to stand behind the quality of your products, any products are below the satisfactory standard are automatically eliminated.
- Core values educate clients and potential customers about what the organization is all about and clarify the identity of the organization. In this competitive world, when you have a set of specific values that speak out to the public, that is definitely a competitive advantage.
- Core values are becoming primary recruiting and retention tools. With the ease of researching organizations, job seekers are doing their homework on the identities of the organizations they are applying for and weighing whether or not these organizations hold the values that the job seekers consider as important.

So, let's take some examples of these values:

1- The policy of the open door (which means that any employee can meet with the upper management without the permission of his or her immediate supervisor or manager.
2- It could be transparency in work which means that there are no secrets and everything is recorded and obvious for everybody.
3- Some values could be the *market share* like to dominate this percent of the market share is one of our values.

How do we scan the values or how do we identify the values?

Individual values:

These are the values that are related to the founders of the organization, decision-makers, and planning team.

Founders of the organization, decision-makers, and planning team, write down the values that they would like to adopt in the organization, then they vote on the best values to be adopted.

Organizational values:

After voting on the individual values, the agreed-upon values will be adopted to become the values of the organization. And that will affect what can and cannot be done within the organization.

For example: if one of these values was to focus on having more market share than the profit margin that will affect all the decisions in the organization.

Organizational philosophy:

The statement of philosophy is defined as an explanation of the systems of beliefs that determine how an organization functions and operates. An organization's philosophy states the beliefs, concepts, and principles of an organization.

How to write the values?

- As a start the founders of the organization in case they are in the phase of establishing this organization they should write down the values that they want to implement and grow in their organization.
- We ask the planning team ahead of time of the meeting of identifying the values, to write down individually the values that they think the organization should implement and the values that should be eliminated in case it was an already established organization.
- Then at the time of the meeting, we present these values which the planning team has already written down.
- The values that are repeated by many individuals from the planning team we adopt and the values which haven't been repeated we discuss and vote.
- Write the statement of the organizational philosophy.

Another way to write the values:

- We ask the planning team and the decision-makers or the founders to have a meeting, then we do brainstorming and write down all the values that they come up with, then we discuss them and vote for the most important ones.

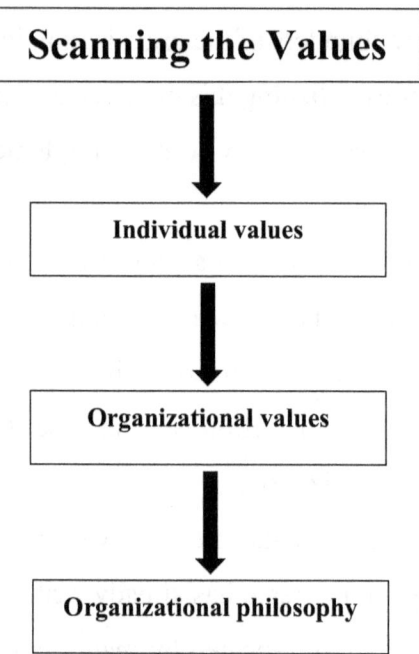

3- The Vision - Step 3

Now we have our planning team and we have our values identified, we need to start to form our vision.

What is the vision?

A Vision is a description of an organization's or individual's desired future state. The vision frames a future position or image and provides a constant reference point for the organization's mission and goals.

In other words, **a vision**: is a desired imaginary image or state for the organization at a certain point in the future.

The purpose of the vision:

A clear vision should bring purpose to everyone in the organization. A vision provides the big picture for anything the organization does. In the process of accomplishing the mission and the goals of the organization, teams can lose sight of the big picture or the purpose for everything they are doing, a vision keeps people focused and provides a reference point for the entire organization.

The vision must become the culture of the organization

A vision should answer the following questions:

- Why are we doing this?
- What is the purpose?

How to write the vision.

1st Step

To write the vision the planning team should specify the main group of questions to come up with the right vision. Keeping in mind that the answers to these questions should be for the end of the timeframe of the strategic plan.

As we mentioned before:

Small organizations for 5 years.

Medium organizations for 10 years.

Large organizations for 15 – 20 years.

Some of these questions which work well with most types of organization are:

We can always start these questions, according to your organization size, with the phrase:

After (5 years, 10 years, 15 or 20 years)

1- How many employees should we have at the end of our plan?
2- How many branches?
3- What is my order among my competitors?
4- What are the most important products or services that we provide?
5- What are the most important division (how are our division categorized? according to the product and service or geographically, or financially or structurally).
6- What is our income?
7- What is the profit ratio to the income?

8- What kind of technology we are using? This question is connected to the number of employee's questions putting into consideration that *with the use of the technology the number of employees should decrease.*

And of course, any other question that would be suitable according to the type of your organization.

2nd Step

Planning team members answer these questions **individually** then they bring the answers with them to the next meeting.

A good practice to do is writing these questions and any others you might feel good to your organization and send them to the planning team and give them a period of time to answer them **individually**, then take all of their answers and send them out collectively to all of the planning team members, so they will know the answers of all the members before the next appointed meeting to save time.

3rd Step

At the time of the meeting after we got and distributed all the answers, we present all the answers in front of the planning team in the meeting on a slide on a big screen where we categorize the human resources answers together and the financial answers together and the business essence answers together, and so on.

4th Step

All the answers that are similar and agreed upon we put them as agreed upon. In case there is any disagreement on any answers we discuss these answers then we vote and take the majority votes upon the answers until we get to a point that we have agreed upon all answers to all the questions that we put.

Once we have agreed upon the answers to all of these questions, we have a vision of where our organization will be in the future and we can adequately put all these answers and phrase them to present our vision.

5th Step

An additional step but it is not a necessity, (Summarize the vision in a statement) so it will stick in the mind of all the employees.

4- The Mission - Step 4

A mission statement is a brief description of an organization's fundamental purpose.

And it answers 2 questions:

1- who are we?
2- And, what do we want?

Writing the Mission Statement.

To write a good Mission statement you need to take into consideration the following qualities:

The Qualities of the Mission statement:

1- To be obvious and easy to understand.
2- To be brief and short easy to memorize. It's better to be no more than 20 words, the more you can shorten it the better.
3- Describes the organization by answering the following: (who, what, why, where)
   - A- Who are you? (means what do you do.)
   - B- Who is your audience?
   - C- What product or service do you provide?
   - D- Why are you distinguished?
   - E- Where do you operate?
4- Focus on one strategic major aspect. Or what business are you in?
5- What makes you unique from your competitors? (the best the first – the second- the best quality)
6- To be broad but not vague and specific without details.

7- To be a reference point for the decisions in the organization.
8- Reflect the values of the organization. (no more than 3 values in the mission statement)
9- Reflects achievable goals during the period of the plan.
10- Makes you proud.

After knowing the qualities of the mission statement, ask your planning team as we did in writing the vision, ask them all to write a statement individually then assign a meeting and present all of them and discuss and vote to come up with the desired mission statement.

Let's have few examples:

McDonald's Mission Statement

Our aim is to provide a fun and safe environment where our customers can enjoy good food made with quality ingredients at affordable prices.

Apple's mission statement

Apple designs Macs, the best personal computers in the world, along with OS X, iLife, iWork and professional software. Apple leads the digital music revolution with its iPods and iTunes online store. Apple has reinvented the mobile phone with its revolutionary iPhone and App Store, and is defining the future of mobile media and computing devices with iPad.

Starbucks's mission statement:

To inspire and nurture the human spirit – one person, one cup and one neighborhood at a time.

Apply the mission qualities to the previous statements and see if they are missing something.

Strategic business model

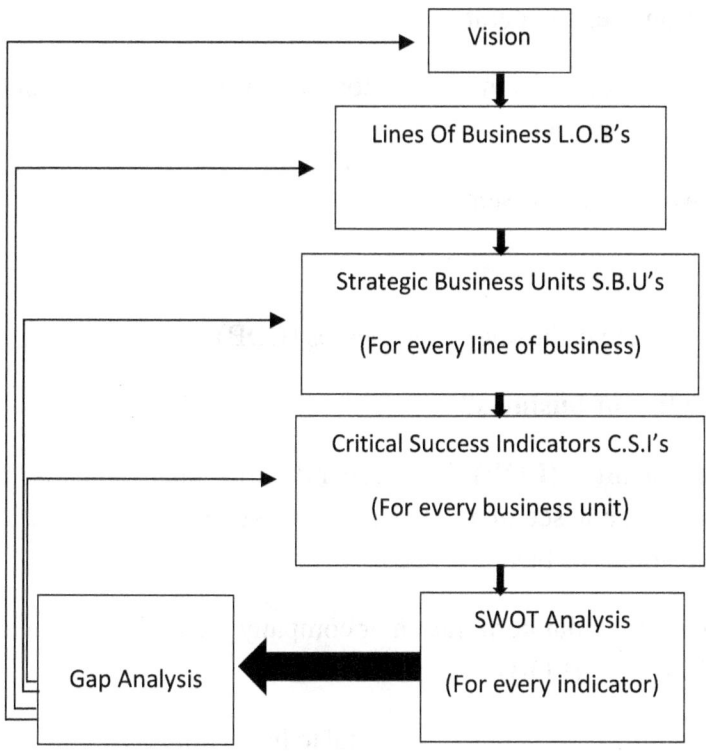

5- Strategic business model - Step 5

A strategic business model is simply the method and strategy that an organization uses to operate.

After we had our vision ready, now we want to identify our strategic business model.

To do that we have a few steps

Step A:

Identify the line of business/ businesses (LOB).

What is the line of business?

Line of business (LOB) is a general term that refers to a product/service or a set of related products/services that serve a particular customer or business need.

If you have a regular corporation or company most likely to have one line of business (LOB)

But for holding companies it is normal to have more than one line of business.

An important note:

According to *Porter,* you should not have more than 3 related lines of businesses under one company.

That means you can't be a marketing company and have a restaurant and a retail store as 3 different LOBs under the same company, But you can as a marketing company, for example, to have 3 LOBs like let's say LOB 1 social media marketing, LOB 2 web design and development, LOB 3 marketing consultant. These 3 LOBs are related in one way or another so you can have them all under one company.

Step B:

Identify the strategic business unit/ units (SBU).

Strategic business unit (SBU): is any division from the essence of the business that can operate independently with responsibility for a particular range of products or services.

That means that the SBU has its own plan, its own budget, and its own management.

For example:

We have an education organization, under this organization, we have a training line of business and we do training in sales, marketing, and management.

We can take our sales training part of the business and make it as a strategic business unit SBU and open a center only for sales training, this SBU will have its own plan, its own budget, and its own management. In this case, this sales training center will be the first SBU under the LOB, and if we open another sales training center will be the second SBU under the LOB.

There is no limit for the number of the Strategic Business Units SBUs under each LOB as long as the part of the business can be independent. From our example above you can have an unlimited number of sales training centers under the Training Line of Business.

Support unit:

We also have the **Support unit:** a support unit is every department that supports our business. like the finance department, the legal department, the procurement department, and the IT department, etc.

For these departments we **cannot** make them as SBUs because they are not from the essence of our business as of our example above, we work in education and these departments are only to support our business.

We can make the support unit central or we can create a support unit for each strategic business unit SBU if needed.

The rule for this whenever an SBU needs an employee full time like finance, legal, IT, or procurement, etc. we give them that employee and make it a support unit for that SBU under their control, but if the SBU doesn't need these employees as full time at that time we can make the support unit central. We can apply the same thing to the LOBs.

See the diagram on the next page:

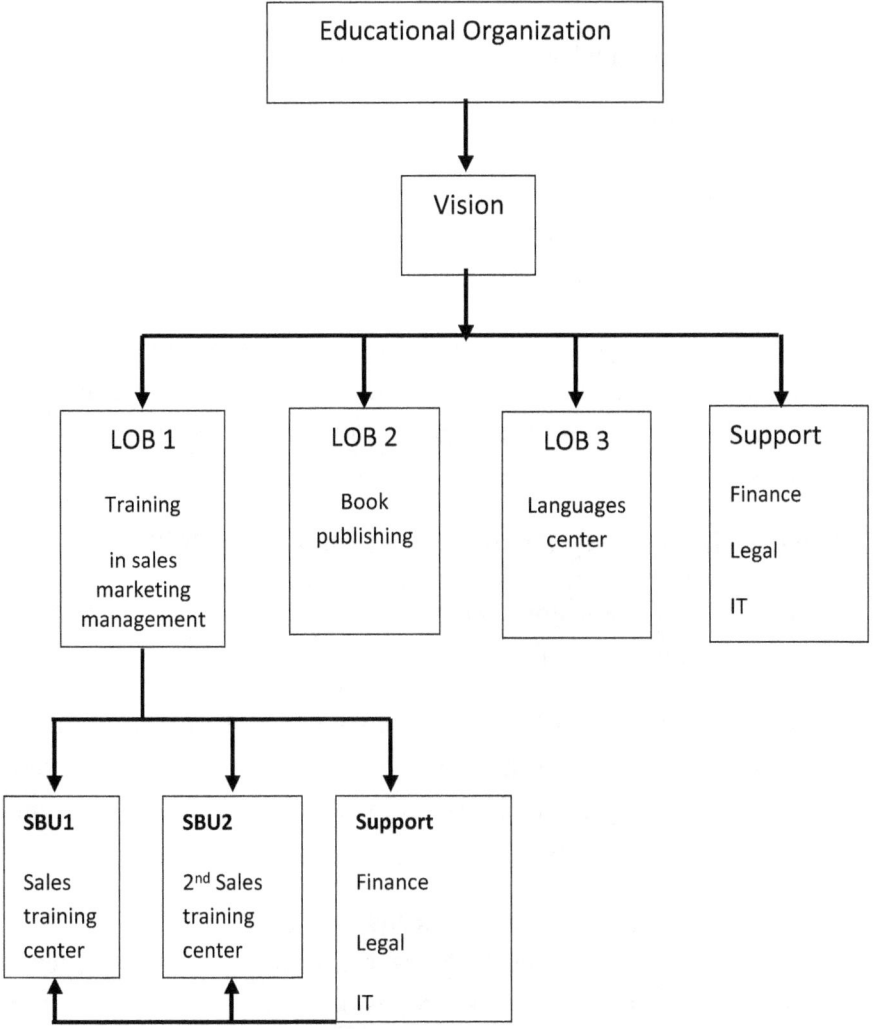

Step C:

Identify the critical success indicators.

Critical Success indicators

In the world of management, we have many indicators and factors to measure the performance of the organizations and we call them critical success indicators

The most popular one is KPI Key Performance Indicator, most of the organizations use the KPI's to measure and keep tracking the performance according to their plan, and this is what we are going to focus on.

The definition of Key Performance Indicator, or KPI:

A KPI is an indicator that specifies the minimum acceptable amount of achievement for a certain goal.

KPI is a measure of performance within an organization, to evaluate the success of the business according to its primary objectives or strategic plan. KPIs vary widely, depending on the type of business and its goals.

KPIs are the measurable means of the leadership of any organization to evaluate the progress toward its short and long-term goals. We can set KPIs for a short period of time and KPIs for the whole period of the plan.

It is recommended that every SBU to have at least 3 KPI and no more than 10 KPI's so it could be realistic.

Let's take an example to understand KPI better:

An X car dealership sets a KPI of selling 12000 cars in the next coming 5 years.

That means selling 12000 cars is the minimum acceptable amount of sales that this dealership must achieve in 5 years, so let's say that after 5 years this dealership sold 15000 cars, that would be great because they exceeded their minimum goal of 12000 cars, but if they sold less than 12000 car that means that the management is not good and an action should be taken.

This is why we set short term KPIs so we can measure in the short run and adjust to avoid getting behind our desired goal on the period of our plan.

For the same example this dealership must sell 12000 cars in 5 years in this case we set a KPI for this year where we divide the 12000 / 5 = 2400 unit or car, in this case, we can measure the performance in one year to do any necessary action in case we could not achieve the minimum goal (KPI) of this year so we can adjust our plan accordingly.

Of course, this is just a simple example to understand the idea, this is why we divided the targeted sales number into 5 years, but what really happens is every year our sales should be increasing and every year we should have a growth over the year before.

We can have many Key performance indicators in any of the following perspectives according to our organization type:

- Finance perspective.

- Customer perspective.

- Operation perspective.

- Sales perspective.

- Marketing perspective.

- Environment perspective.

- Information technology perspective.

We can say for example:

- We want our client's number to be 500 clients (client KPI is 500 Clients).
- Our order fulfillment is no more than 1 hour.
- Our revenue per employee is $X amount of money.
- Our cost of lead is no more than $X amount of money.

So back to our strategic business model, after we had our vision ready then we identified our (LOB) Line of Business, then we created our SBUs strategic business units, then we sat our goals for the SBUs which means our KPIs the key performance indicators.

Now the fourth step.

Management for Entrepreneurs

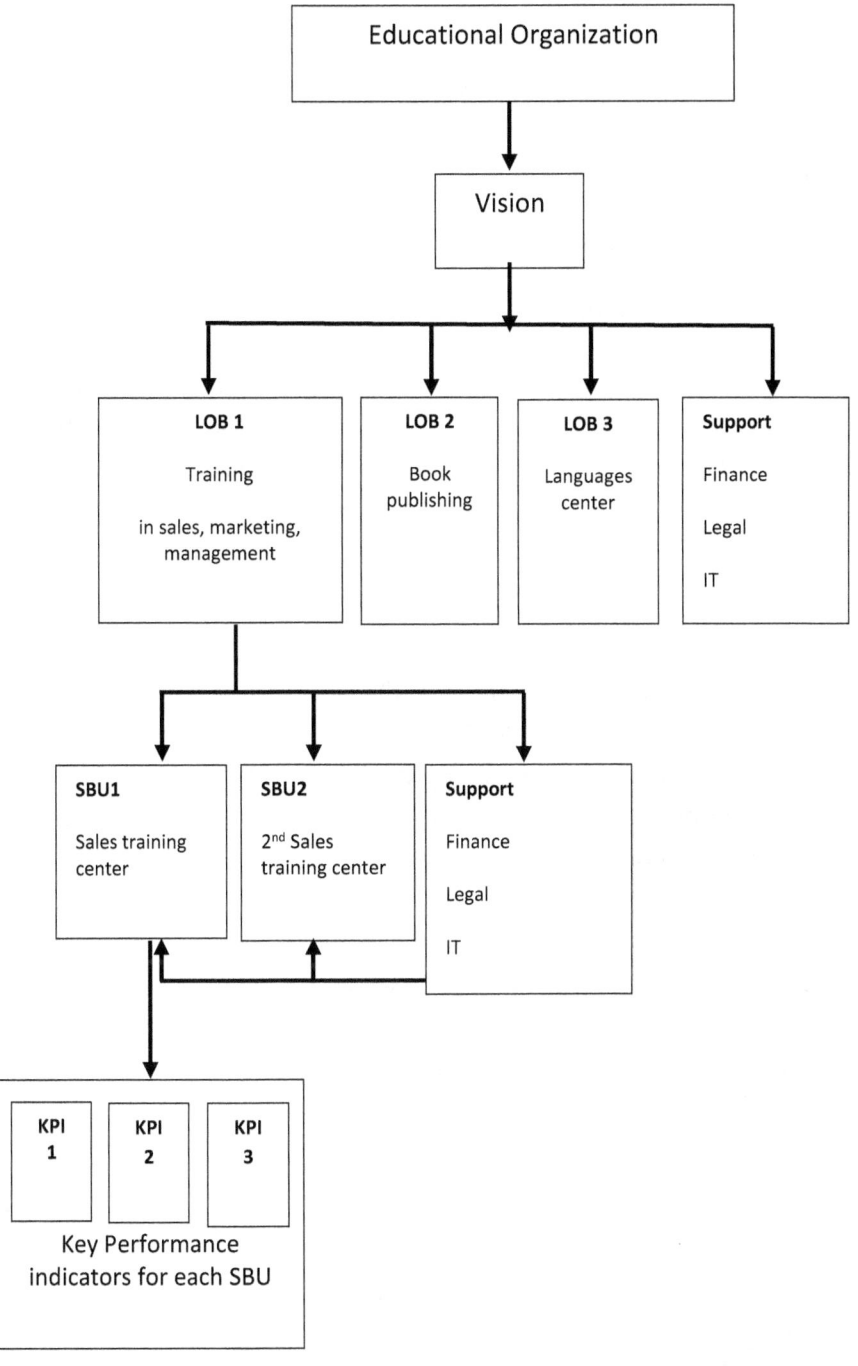

Step D:

Strategic thrust: is a set of actions to achieve a set of goals in a strategy, it sets out what you need to do or execute to achieve a strategic goal.

Each thrust focuses on a specific business need.

For example (equipment, systems, processes, administrations, etc.)

Each thrust discussion starts with a paragraph giving a general background on the thrust. A brief statement of the "business need". After listing the thrust's objective, the thrust discussion concludes with a list of "building blocks" (i.e., products or processes that must be available to satisfy the business need).

In few words Strategic thrust is the tools you need to conduct the business to achieve your strategic goals, it might be establishing an HR department for your strategic business unit SBU, accounting system, computers for each employee, and an IT system, to achieve your goals according to your key performance indicators KPIs.

Example:

We are creating a new sales unit sales SBU under our LOB.

What do we need to establish this unit?

    Thrust 1: an HR department for this unit

    Thrust 2: computers and sales software

    Thrust 3: accounting department for this unit.

    Etc.....

Thrust 1 objectives:

Create an HR department for the new strategic business unit (the new sales unit) within 30 days

Building blocks:

1- Hire HR employees.

2- Purchase computers and software for the HR dept.

3- Develop policies and procedures.

4- Training HR employees.

5- Etc.

This was just a simple example to understand the strategic thrust.

Step E:

Organizational culture: is the underlying beliefs, values, and assumptions that govern the way people performing their roles in an organization.

Every organization develops and maintains a unique culture, which provides guidelines and boundaries for the behavior of the employees of the organization.

When you have a strong organizational culture, you will enjoy the following:

- Employees will know how the leadership of an organization wants them to respond to any situation.
- Define the proper way for the employees to behave within the organization.
- Shaping employee's perceptions, behaviors, and understanding.

Types of organizational structure:

According to Robert E. Quinn and Kim S. Cameron at the University of Michigan at Ann Arbor, there are four types of organizational culture: Clan, Adhocracy, Market, and Hierarchy.

- **Clan** oriented cultures are family-like, with a focus on mentoring, nurturing, and "doing things together."

- **Adhocracy** oriented cultures are dynamic and entrepreneurial, with a focus on risk-taking, innovation, and "doing things first."

- **Market**-oriented cultures are results-oriented, with a focus on competition, achievement, and "getting the job done."

- **Hierarchy** oriented cultures are structured and controlled, with a focus on efficiency, stability, and "doing things right."

There's no correct organizational culture for an organization. All cultures promote some forms of behavior and inhibit others. Some are well suited to rapid and repeated change; others are suited to slow incremental development of the institution.

According to Quinn and Cameron associate the lower two cultures (Hierarchy and Market) with a principal focus on stability and the upper two (Clan and Adhocracy) with flexibility and adaptability. A Hierarchy culture based on Control will lead mainly to incremental change, while a focus on Adhocracy will more typically lead to breakthrough change.

The right culture will be the one that closely fits the direction and strategy of a particular organization as it confronts its own issues and the challenges of a particular time.

What culture do you want for your organization and how could you move towards it in the future?

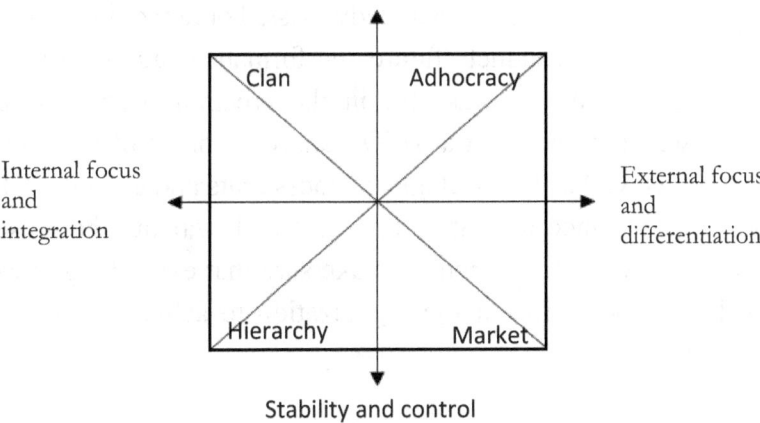

- the dynamic, entrepreneurial Create Culture. (**Adhocracy**)
- the people-oriented, friendly Collaborate Culture. (**Clan**)
- the process-oriented, structured Control Culture. (**Hierarchy**)
- the results-oriented, competitive Compete Culture. (**Market**)

6- Performance audit - Step 6

After the planning team has articulated the desired future state for the organization and laid out the strategic business model. It's time to examine the present state for the changes that have been done to the organization if it was an already existed organization or to set the structure to conduct future performance audits for the organization in case it was still in the creation phase. A very effective way is to conduct a SWOT analysis for all of the line of businesses as well as the strategic business units and even the KPIs the key performance indicators to assess and evaluate the present situation for each one of them to make sure that everything is well aligned with the vision of the organization to achieve its desired future state.

SWOT analysis

What is a SWOT analysis?

SWOT analysis is a study undertaken by an organization to identify its internal and external strengths and weaknesses, as well as its opportunities and threats.

SWOT analysis is an effective way to analyze the present situation of an organization or any unit within the organization where it can provide you with the analysis you need to make a plan to achieve the desired situation for it.

SWOT stands for the initial of the following words:

S	Strengths	Points of strengths
W	Weaknesses	Points of weaknesses
O	Opportunities	Available opportunities
T	Threats	Expected threats

To understand our present situation, we need to analyze:

1- Strengths: our strength points that we already have **NOW**.

2- Weakness: our weakness points that we already have **NOW**.

3- Opportunities: opportunities that we can, with some endeavors and efforts, to achieve within the period of time of the plan in the **FUTURE**.

4- Threats: the expected threats that we might have in the **FUTURE** and work on avoiding them.

Strengths	NOW
Weaknesses	
Opportunities	FUTURE
Threats	

Some people divide these 4 factors into:

Internal (strengths and weaknesses).

External (opportunities and threats).

And that is **WRONG** because we can have external (strengths and weaknesses)

And we can have internal (opportunities and threats).

Let's take an example:

Strengths	Weaknesses
1- We have a high-quality product (internal). 2- We have a big client base (external). 3- We have a great leader (internal). **Now**	1- Our budget is not enough (internal). 2- Our competitor created a product better than our product (external). 3- Our team spirit is not good (internal). **Now**
Opportunities	**Threats**
1- Open a new branch within a year (external). 2- Develop our team skills to provide new services to our clients (internal). **Future**	1- New government regulation could affect our business (external). 2- Our great leader could leave our organization (internal). **Future**

It is recommended to have no less than 3 Strengths and no more than ten.

No less than 3 weaknesses and no more than 10.

No less than 1 opportunity and no more than 3 to be realistic.

No less than 1 threat and no more than 3 to be realistic.

Strengths	**Weaknesses**
No less than 3 strengths to 10 strengths maximum	No less than 3 weaknesses to 10 weaknesses maximum
Opportunities	**Threats**
No less than 1 strength to 3 strengths maximum	No less than 1 weakness to 3 weaknesses maximum

Now when you analyze the strengths, weaknesses, opportunities, and threats you will have a clear insight of what is your current situation so you can work on your operational plan to set your goals, and this is what we are going to learn later in details in the operational plan chapter in this book so we can apply it to this step after we conduct our present analysis (SWOT analysis).

7- Gap analysis - Step 7

A gap analysis is a process used to identify gaps that are existed between the current and the desired situations in an organization.

When we are talking about the gap analysis for an organization, we are looking to identify the gap which is the space between "where we are" and "where we want to be" to find the right path to get to "where we want to be".

Before you can do a gap analysis, you must know the desired outcomes. These outcomes are clearly identified in the KPIs and when you do a SWOT analysis to create your operational plan you will have your goals identified clearly and in the next chapter, we will learn exactly how to write our goals from SWOT analysis.

Let's see a sample of the gap analysis matrix to have a better understanding:

Sample Gap Analysis Matrix

Issue	Desired outcome	Why it is happening
Not producing enough products to meet the demand (current production 300 units a day)	Produce 500 units a day	Production is processed manually
Employment turnover increased by 10% now.	Keep it less than 3%	Our competitor is offering 4 days 10 hours a day per week. Our employees leaving us to them.
fulfillment time increased 25%, it is 1 hour and 15 minutes now	Keep it 1-hour product fulfillment time.	2 fulfillment employees have quit.

From this gap analysis matrix, we can know:

- What is the problem?
- What is the desired outcome?
- What causes the problem?

Now after we identified the gaps, we can think of the solutions to bridge the gap between the current situation and the desired one and set our goals accordingly.

CHAPTER 3

OPERATIONAL PLANNING

OPERATIONAL PLANNING

8- Integrating action Plan - Step 8

The creation of the operational plan.

As a start in this step, we need to know how to set a SMART Goal to be able to integrate our action plan or create our operational plan.

So, let's get started.

Setting SMART Goals or Objectives:

Having vague goals will not lead you to any desired outcome in the future, this is why goals should be very clear and measurable.

Remember this rule:

If you can't measure it, you can't manage it.

So, what makes goals achievable and easier to lead us to the desired outcomes.

In management we set our goals to be SMART, what do we mean by SMART goals!?

The word SMART stands for the initials of the following words

SMART				
S	M	A	R	T
Specific	Measurable	Agreed upon	Realistic	Time framed
What is the specific desired result?	It should be measured in a reliable way	Agreed upon the goal between the planner and the executor	Within reach, not impossible to achieve, and relevant to the main purpose	Has a limited period of time. Has a deadline to achieve.

Let's take an example:

The management of a mobile phone factory which produces 750 phones per day decided to increase production.

Vague goal: increase our production

SMART goal: increase our mobile phone production to produce 1000 units per day using 20 employees within 30 days.

We find in this SMART goal example:

The goal is Specific: increase phone production to 1000 units per day using 20 employees. (very specific they specified the amount of unit production and how many employees to do that).

The goal is Measurable: increase phone production to 1000 units per day using 20 employees. (you can measure how many units should be produced every day with how many employees and how long you need to get there "30 days").

The goal is Agreed upon: when the planning team set this goal, they should agree with the production management that this goal is ok and they can do it.

The goal is Realistic: it should be hard but not impossible, that means that the factory should have within reach all the means to increase the production from 750 units a day to 1000 units per day, they might need to hire more staff if they have less than 20 as mention in the goal or they might have the 20 employees but they need to do more overtime or they might need to add more machinery to the product line. This is why the executor and the planner should agree upon the goal to get the needed means to achieve that and the time frame needed to do that.

The goal is time-framed: they specified the time frame to achieve this goal is 30 days.

Now we understood how to set a smart goal let's see how to handle this goal and make it easy to achieve.

The Goal Table:

For every SMART goal we set, we create a table as the following:

Date: Dec-25th			
Goal: increase our mobile phone production to produce 1000 units per day using 20 employees within 30 days.			
Means	Who	When (deadline)	Cost
1- Decide what kind of machinery we need.	David (procurement)	Jan 1st	$0
2- Purchasing the needed machinery	David (procurement)	Jan 5th	$5,000
3- Hire 5 more employees (1supervisor + 1packaging + 3 assemblers)	Tom (HR)	Jan 5th	$15,500
4- Create a new shift for the new employees.	Tom (HR)	Jan 5th	$0
5- Train the new employees	Mark (operations)	Jan 24th	$0

This is how we work every SMART goal we have.

OPERATIONAL PLANNING

What is an operational plan?

An Operational Plan is short term plan which is usually has a one-year period of time and it is a highly detailed plan that provides a clear picture of how a team, section, or department will contribute to achieve the organization's goals. The operational plan maps out the day-to-day tasks required to run a business.

The plan covers the what, the who, the when, and how much:

What - the tasks to be achieved or completed.

Who - the individuals who have the responsibility to achieve each task.

When - the timeline for the tasks that Should be completed.

How much – the financial resources available or needed to complete the tasks.

How do we do the operational plan?

Step 1: We conduct a SWOT analysis:

As we learn earlier in this book SWOT analysis is a study undertaken by an organization to identify its internal and external strengths and weaknesses, as well as its opportunities and threats.

In this step, we conduct a SWOT analysis to identify our:

- Strengths.
- Weaknesses.
- Opportunities.
- Threats.

Step 2: Form our SMART Goals from the SWOT analysis.

After we have our SWOT analysis ready, our task now is to make every strength point, weakness point, opportunity, and threat, as a SMART goal for our plan.

How?

In Strengths:

Our goal is to maintain or increase our strength points and form them as SMART goals as we've learned earlier when we talked about the SMART goals.

In Weaknesses:

Our goal is to enhance and improve our weakness points until they become strength points, and form them as SMART goals.

In Opportunities:

Our goal is to work on achieving these opportunities during the period of the plan since the opportunity is something good that we can achieve with effort.

In Threats:

Our goal is to be prepared to avoid the threat points and form them as SMART goals.

Let's take a look at the following random example of what a SWOT analysis might be.

SWOT analysis:

Strengths	Weaknesses
1- We have a high-quality product. 2- We have a big client base. 3- We have a great leader.	1- Team skills are weak and not up to date. 2- Our competitor created a product better than our product. 3- Our team spirit is not good.
Opportunities	**Threats**
1- Open a new branch within a year. 2- Develop our team skills to provide new services to our clients.	1- New government regulations could affect our business. 2- Our great leader could leave our organization.

Forming our SMART Goals:

Goals:

In strengths:

Goals in strengths	
Strength points	1- We have a high-quality product.
Change into a SMART goal	1- Maintaining our product's high-quality, by doing a monthly quality training session for 3 hours on our quality criteria, to our production team, and conduct a daily random quality testing for the raw materials and the final product, throughout the year.

And keep going till we finish all of our strength points.

Goals:

In weaknesses:

Goals in weaknesses	
weakness points	1- Team skills are weak and not up to date.
Change into a SMART goal	1- Conduct 3 training courses for our 150 employees 2 courses in their main domain and one general course in business, one course every 4 months to keep them up to date with all new technology and trends in our line of business, every year.

And keep going till we finish all of our weakness points.

Goals:

In opportunities:

Goals in opportunities	
opportunities	1- Open a new branch within a year.
Change into a SMART goal	1- Open a new branch in the city of Orange California with 150 employees by December

And keep going till we finish all of our opportunities.

Goals:

In threats:

Goals in threats	
Threats	1- Our great leader could leave our organization.
Change into a SMART goal	1- Conduct 3 training courses, one on leadership and one on how to become a CEO and one by our CEO to prepare a replacement for him to 3 of our employees (our vice president, our CFO, and our COO) by the end of the year to avoid the threat of our CEO leaving us.

And keep going till we finish all of our threats.

Step 3- Creating the goal table.

For every SMART Goal we have formed from our SWOT analysis, we create a Means Table.

The Means Table provides the what, the who, the when, and how much:

What (the means) - the tasks to be achieved or completed.

Who - the individuals who have the responsibility to achieve each task.

When - the timeline for the tasks that Should be completed.

How much – the financial resources available or needed to complete the tasks.

For example, let's put our following SMART goal into the means table

Goals in strengths	
Strength points	1- We have a high-quality product.
Change into a SMART goal	1- Maintaining our product's high-quality, by doing a monthly quality training session for 3 hours on our quality criteria, to our production team, and conduct a daily random quality testing for the raw materials and the final product, throughout the year.

THE GOAL TABLE

Date: Dec-25th

Goal: Maintaining our product's high-quality, by doing a monthly quality training session for 3 hours on our quality criteria, to our production team, and conduct a daily random quality testing for the raw materials and the final product, throughout the year.

What (The Means)	Who	When (deadline)	Cost
1- Prepare the monthly quality criteria training material.	Sam (quality manager)	By the 15th of every month	$300 per month
2- Inform and remind the production team to attend the training by email.	Mary (admin assistant)	First reminder 26th of every month. Second reminder 28th of every month.	$0
3- Book the conference room for the training	Mary (admin assistant)	29th of every month	$0
4- Conduct the training for the production team	Sam (quality manager)	29th of every month at 5:00 pm	3 hours overtime by the number of employees
5- conduct a daily random quality testing for the raw materials	Sam (quality manager)	Every day at 8:30 Am	$0
6- conduct a daily random quality testing for the final product	Sam (quality manager)	Every day at 3:00 pm	$0
7- prepare a weekly quality test result report and send it to the upper management by email.	Sam (quality manager)	Every Thursday at 2:00 pm	$0

Now we can see how we changed the SMART goal into action.

Step 4- The Time Table.

After we have done the goal table for every goal and we identified the following clearly:

What (the means) - the tasks to be achieved or completed.

Who - the individuals who have the responsibility to achieve each task.

When - the timeline for the tasks that Should be completed.

How much (the cost) – the financial resources available or needed to complete the tasks.

It is time now to make our time table, to arrange these tasks in a timely manner along the period of the plan (1 year).

How do we do the time table?

To do the time table we make the following table for every month of the year:

The Time Table for January year XXXX			
What (the means)	**Who**	**When**	**How much (the cost)**
1- Prepare the monthly quality criteria training material.	Sam (quality manager)	By the 15th of every month	$300 per month
2- Inform and remind the production team to attend the training by email.	Mary (admin assistant)	First reminder 26th of every month

Second reminder 28th of every month. | $0 |
Total cost of the month			Sum of all amounts

The Time Table for February year XXXX			
What (the means)	**Who**	**When**	**How much (the cost)**
3- Prepare a Facebook ad to generate 1000 lead.	Marketing department	5th of February	$0
4- Lunch a social media marketing campaign on Facebook to generate 1000 leads	Marketing department	6th of February	$1000
Total cost of the month			Sum of all amounts

Then we copy all the tasks that should be done in January from the goal tables that we have done in step 3 and put them all in the time table of January, then we put all the tasks we find in the goal tables that must be done on February, and put them all on February time table, and so on until we have all the tasks from the goal tables distributed accordingly on the time tables of every month of the year.

Important Note: the monthly Time Table will allow the management to know their budget for the month because, at the bottom of each month time table, you can calculate the sum of all amounts of the expenditures for that month, and you can know with one glance how much money you're going to spend at that month of the year.

Step 5- The Task Table.

After we have done our monthly time tables for every month of the year, we need to do the task tables to distribute them to every department or individual who is responsible for doing a certain task.

So, every department/individual will know all of the tasks which are required to accomplish along the period of the plan (one year), in one single table.

How to do the Task Table?

To do the task table we need to make the following:

Check all the monthly time tables and see the **who** column and create the following table for all the listed names (departments/individuals) on the Time tables.

The Task Table for the marketing department		
What (the means)	When	How much (the cost)
1- Promote the business on social media. 2-	January	$1000
1-Prepare a Facebook ad to generate 1000 lead. 2- Lunch a social media marketing campaign on Facebook to generate 1000 leads	1-5th of February 2-6th of February	1-$0 2-$1000
A- Promote new service on social media	1-2nd of March	1-$XXX
	April	
	May	
	June	
	July	
	August	
	September	
	October	
	November	
	December	
Total cost		Sum of all amounts

Then every department can do the following table for its individuals:

\	The Task Table for Sam the operation manager	
What (the means)	When	How much (the cost)
1- 2- 3- 4-	January	1- $300 2- $0 3- $500 4- $700
1- 2-	February	
	March	
	April	
	May	
	June	
	July	
	August	
	September	
	October	
	November	
	December	
Total cost		Sum of all amounts

Now we have done all of our work and we have our operational plan ready.

So, basically for the management of the organization, they need to have only the monthly TIME TABLES and the TASK TABLE for every party responsible for doing a task.

From the monthly **Time Table,** the management will know exactly what should be done at that month and what are the costs for every task in that month and who is doing the task.

From the **Task Table,** the management of the organization will know exactly every department and individual who is responsible for doing a task, what that task is, and what goals they should achieve and what are the costs for their tasks all over the year.

So, once we have the time tables and the task tables, we distribute them to the management, departments, and individuals who are involved and we have our operational plan for the year done.

9- Coordination of action/operational plan - Step 9

What do we mean by the coordination of the integrated action or operational plan?

Simply the planning team take another look at the operational plan and start to do the coordination by distributing the tasks and the cost on the months of the year in a way that makes the work easy where we don't have very busy months and some with very light tasks to do, and some months with a lot of expenses and some months with very light expenses.

In other words, the planning team tries to move the tasks from the very busy months to other months with less or little tasks to do.

In this case, we will have a smooth work operation and we will not have problems with the cash flow.

Although this step looks simple, but it has a great effect on the plan and the smoothness of the work process.

10- Contingency planning - Step 10

A contingency plan is a course of actions designed to help an organization to respond effectively to a significant future event or situation, where this event or situation could have a huge effect on the organization's future in a bad or even in a good way.

A contingency plan is sometimes referred to as "Plan B," because it can be also used as alternative actions if the expected results fail to materialize.

When the planning team writes down the strategic plan for an organization, they put in mind things with a very low possibility to happen but if they do happen, they would hugely affect the organization, so the planning team creates the contingency plan to outline the actions that the organization should do in case something like that happens.

For example:

School districts in America when the Coronavirus COVID19 spread, they closed some schools to avoid the spread of the virus among the students and their families, if you think about it how rare is the possibility to have a plague or a fatal virus to spread in a country like the USA in such a scary way. But they have in their contingency plan that in case something like this happens they were prepared and they outlined what is the contingency plan for this possibility and they change their plan and closed the schools in the affected areas and transfer to online teaching, so instead of students go to school, they can attend the school classes online on their computer at home.

Contingency plans will also outline the actions for the things which have a very low possibility but if they happen the organization will have huge profits.

Usually, the planning team doesn't make a contingency plan for every possibility rather than what we mentioned before, only the things that might hugely affect the organization, and they only put the big outlines they don't go into details, and in case something happens they have the outlines and the indicators for the situation and can make their plan in a very little time.

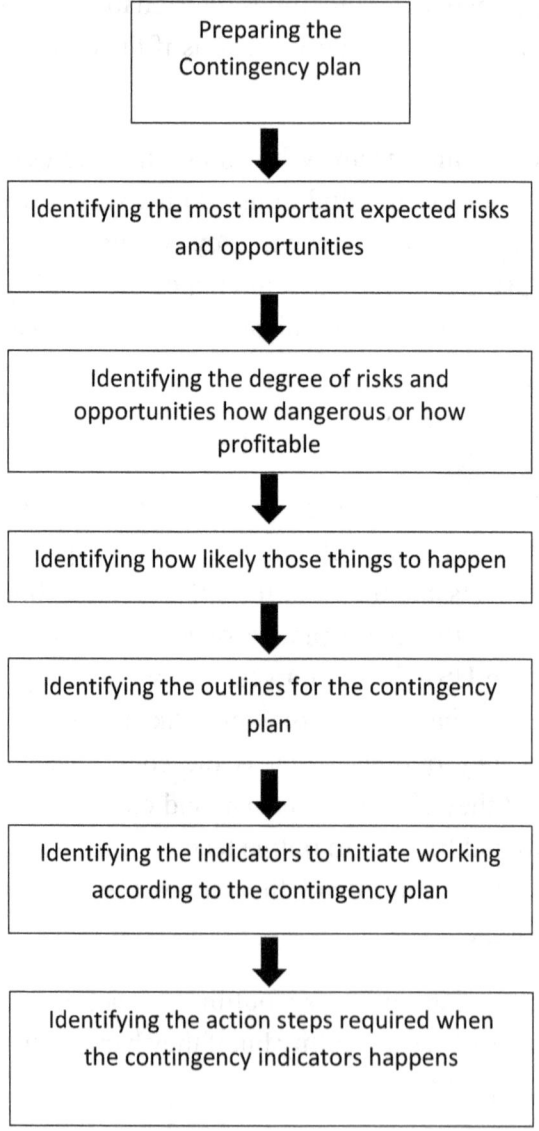

11- Plan implementation - Step 11

Implementation is *the process that converts strategies and plans into actions to achieve strategic objectives and goals*. Implementing is as important, or even more important, than your strategy.

The strategic plan mainly focuses on the **what** and **why** of activities, but implementation focuses on the **who, where, when,** and **how**.

Having the strategic plan is like you finished from the base structure of the building and the rest is the implementation so none of them has any meaning without the other.

Implementation Pitfalls

To succeed in implementing your strategic plan avoid the following:

Here are some of the most common reasons strategic plans fail:

- **Lack of communication:** when the plan doesn't get communicated properly to employees, and they don't understand how to contribute.

- **Drowning in the day-to-day activities:** entrepreneurs and managers, who are consumed by daily operating problems and activities, lose sight of long-term goals.

- **Losing track:** when an organization treats the plan as something separate from the management process.

- **An overwhelming plan:** The goals and actions generated in the strategic planning are not realistic which means they are way more than what the organization could handle.

- **A meaningless plan:** The vision, mission, and value statements are viewed as something extra and not supported by actions or failing to make employees believe in them.
- **Lack of strategy discussion:** Strategy is not discussed on monthly basis.
- **Not considering implementation:** The implementation process isn't taken seriously. The planning document is seen as an achievement in itself.
- **No progress report:** when there's no method to track progress.
- **No accountability:** when organizations don't plan the right way and there is no proper way to assign tasks to employees and hold them accountable for those tasks.
- **Lack of empowerment:** accountability may provide strong motivation for improving performance, but employees must also have the authority, responsibilities, and tools necessary to achieve their assigned tasks and goals, otherwise they will lose interest.

Implementation consideration

Implementation consideration Should be in mind all along the process of planning and during the implementation process.

It is good to answer the following questions and keep them in mind all the time:

- How committed are you to implementing the plan to move your organization forward?
- How do you plan to communicate the plan throughout the organization?
- How will you drive people in the organization to believe in the plan to move the organization forward?
- What type of motivation are you going to implement in your organization for your employees?
- Have you identified internal processes to drive the plan forward?
- Are you going to allocate money, resources, and time to support your plan?
- What are the roadblocks or obstacles that you might face to implement and support the plan?
- How will you utilize resources to achieve maximum results with them?

MODULE -2-

ORGANIZING

Chapter 4: Introduction to Organizing Function

Chapter 5: The Process of Organizing

Chapter 6: Organizing Grouping

Chapter 7: Organizing Principles

Chapter 8: Time Management

CHAPTER 4

INTRODUCTION TO ORGANIZING FUNCTION

INTRODUCTION TO ORGANIZING FUNCTION

Organizing is the second function of the management process.

It is the process of establishing an order of the use of all the resources within the organization. It is a combination of time, human, financial, and information resources management has to achieve the organizational goals.

Organizing is essential because it facilitates administration as well as the workflow of the organization.

In planning, we identify where we want to be in the future and how we can get there. In organizing, we decide on the ways and the means which make it easier to achieve what has been planned.

Organizing creates the organizational structure of authorities and responsibilities. It defines the system of relations within the organization.

Organizing focuses on the following process:

- Identifying and grouping the work that needs to be done.
- Defining and determining responsibility and authorities for each position within your organization.
- Establishing a relationship among various job positions.
- Determining detailed rules and regulations of work for individuals and groups in the organization.

In organizing when we have a certain task needs to be done, we decide the best efficient way by determining:

What: resources to be used for this task.

Who: is going to perform that task?

When: the task should be performed.

Where: the task should be performed.

How: the task should be performed.

Benefits of organizing

The benefits of the organizing function are as follows.

- Having harmony at work among departments and individuals to execute tasks and achieve goals, effectively and efficiently.
- Everyone in the organization knows what to do. The tasks and responsibilities of all individuals, departments, and major divisions are clearly understood, as well as the type and limits of authority.
- Organizing creates an environment of coordination and cooperation at all levels of the organization.
- Establishing a formal decision-making structure in the organization. Since all people in the organization hierarchy know their authorities and responsibilities that make the decision-making process easier because we have individuals who are experts in handling tasks related to their jobs or positions.

CHAPTER 5

THE PROCESS OF ORGANIZING

THE PROCESS OF ORGANIZING

Organizing is like planning, you need to apply this process carefully. This process involves determining what type of work needs to be done, assigning tasks, and arranging them in the authority and responsibility framework of your organizational structure. If this process is not conducted well, the results you will have will lose efficiency and effectiveness.

The process of organizing consists of the following five steps:

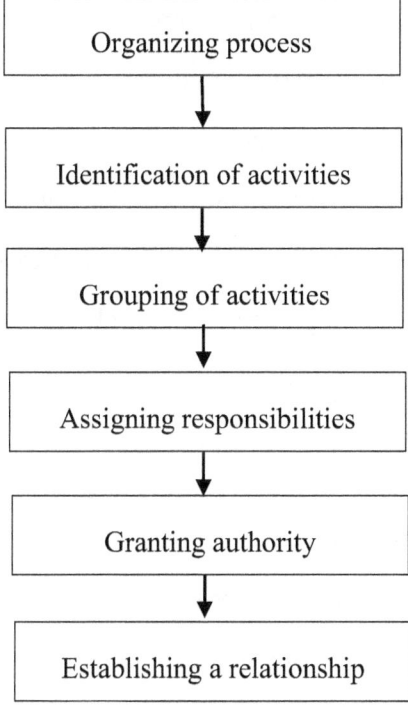

1- Identification of activities.
2- Grouping of activities.
3- Assigning responsibilities.
4- Granting authority.
5- Establishing a relationship.

- **Identification of activities** – Each organization exists to fulfill a specific purpose. This purpose identifies the activities which are conducted by the organization. For example, when we have an educational organization it has different activities and tasks to be done than an organization works in manufacturing. So, we identify the activities that our organization will be involved in. For example, we have an educational organization which creates educational courses, we can identify the activities of this organization as the following:

    - Creating courses.
    - Doing marketing for those courses.
    - Training people to become trainers for those courses.
    - Selling those services (courses & training) to interested educational parties.

- **Grouping of activities** – after identifying the activities, it is very important to put them in groups. So, we can group activities which have similar nature together, that might cause the creation of new departments to serve this purpose.

For example, the activities of the educational organization, related to course creation, from gathering information to preparing the materials to the process of editing can be grouped together and we can create a new department for these activities and call it the course creation department.

- **Assignment of responsibilities** – after completing the first two steps of identifying, and grouping all activities, now it is time to assign these activities or group of activities and tasks to the employees who are going to perform these tasks or activities and hold them responsible and accountable to achieve the desired results.

- **Granting authority** – after assigning tasks and responsibilities you need to support your employees by granting them the authority needed to perform their tasks effectively so they don't struggle and waste time trying to get approvals to do their assigned tasks.

- **Establishing a relationship** – This is a very important part of the organizing function; this is where everyone in the organization knows who reports to whom, and how the relationship among the employees is, to perform their jobs. This establishes the structure of the relationships in the organization and also facilitates the delegation.

Organizing process

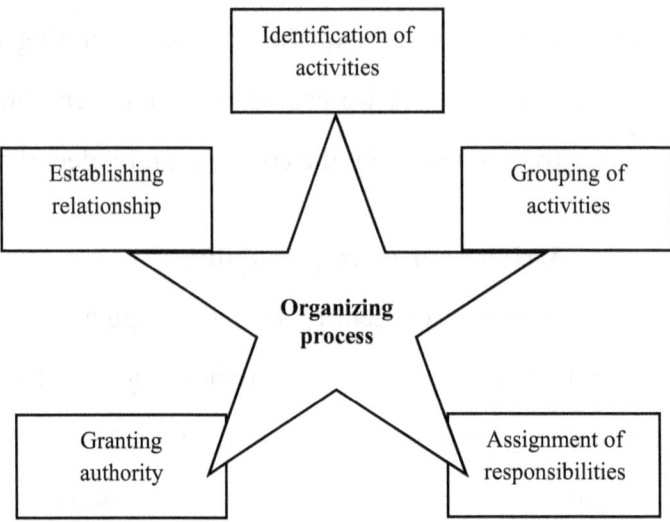

CHAPTER 6

ORGANIZING GROUPING

ORGANIZING GROUPING

Types of grouping activities in organizing function.

Four approaches are usually followed to design the organizational structure of the organization.

- The first approach is the **functional** approach. It is the most common approach. It groups activities according to the function such as sales, marketing, finance, production, and personnel, etc.
- The second approach is the **geographical approach** which groups the activities and responsibilities according to the geographical location. A lot of organizations expand geographically in various parts of the country or even internationally a good example of this type of organization is a franchise organization. Geographic patterns have a direct impact on how organizational activities are to be conducted. Because now we have to deal with many locations and group the activities accordingly. When the organization decides to expand geographically it automatically incurs cost through duplication of employee's positions and the additional building sites needed for the new geographical expansion locations.
- The third approach is the **production line approach**. In this approach, we group activities on a product basis. This approach is normally considered if each product of the

organization needs a unique marketing strategy, production process, distribution system, or capital resources. So instead of grouping the same activities for all of our products, we group the activities specifically to each product. For example, if we are producing electronics and we have a production line for TVs and another production line of air conditioning ACs, we group the marketing activities of the TV production line together, and the marketing activities of the AC production line together, since each production line is unique and has a different strategy. The major disadvantage is similar to the geographic approach which is the additional cost through duplication of the functions within each product line.

- The fourth approach is the **customer approach** which groups activities and resources according to the needs of a specific type of customer group. If customers have a different set of demands, needs, and preferences then, following this approach is appropriate. For example, we are grouping our activities to focus on student customers, so we provide products and services just for the student customer base and we group our activities accordingly.

CHAPTER 7

ORGANIZING PRINCIPLES

ORGANIZING PRINCIPLES

Organizing function in the management process needs to follow some guiding principles to be effective, let's have a quick look at these principles

- **Principle of specialization** – in this principle the organization makes its employees conduct the business according to their specialty and distributes tasks based on its employees' qualifications, abilities, and skills. This is why an effective organization can be achieved by the specialization of dividing work among qualified and skilled employees.
- **Principle of functional definition** – in this principle we define and describe every position in the organization very clearly so managers and employees know exactly what are the responsibilities and authorities of each position in the organization, that facilitates the relationship between management and employees. Clarification in the authority and responsibility helps in making work easier and help in the growth of the organization.
- **Principles of supervision or span of control** – this principle focuses on the number of subordinates that can be managed effectively and efficiently by managers or supervisors in the organization. We have two types; the narrow span of control and the wide span of control. These

two types of spans of control results in either flatter or more hierarchical organizational structure. Let's take a look at the advantages and disadvantages of these two types.

Narrow Span of Control

Advantages:

- Narrow Span of Control has a more hierarchical organization because it has more levels of reporting.
- By having fewer employees' span, supervisors can spend more time with their employees and supervise them more closely.

Disadvantages:

- It is more expensive (high cost of management staff, office, etc.).
- Because of the involvement on the supervisory level in work is more, it could lead to less empowerment and delegation and more micromanagement.
- It causes communication difficulties because of the distance between the top and bottom levels in the organization.

Wide Span of Control

Advantages:

- fewer levels of reporting in the organization, causing a more flexible, flatter organization.
- Supervisors mainly responsible for answering questions, supervising, and helping to solve employees' problems
- Empowering employees by giving more responsibility, delegation, and decision-making power to them.

- **Principle of scalar chain** – it is a formal line of authority that moves from highest to lowest rank in a straight line. every activity in the organization according to this principle must flow according to this chain to have clear communication of orders which is from the higher to the lowest rank in the organization. In this principle, there should be no overlapping of steps during the communication process.

- **Principle of unity of command** – in this principle, one subordinate is accountable to only one supervisor at one time, and the supervisor, in turn, is accountable to only one superior and so on up the organizational hierarchy, even if the top of the organization is led by a group of people. This helps in preventing a lack of communication and feedback and help as well in providing quick responses. This principle leads to effectively combine both physical and financial resources which leads to effective coordination and organizing.

CHAPTER 8
TIME MANAGEMENT

TIME MANAGEMENT

Time is the most wasted resource ever.

We can't actually manage the time because it is out of our control, we can't save it for later, we can't make it faster or we can't make it slower, but what we really can do is to organize and invest our time to get the best out of it.

Time Management also refers to, making the best use of time as time is always limited

Some benefits of time management (organizing):

- Deliver work on time and never being behind.
- Provide a better quality of work and life.
- Having priorities and doing what is more important first.
- Being more productive and efficient.
- Overcome procrastination.
- Less stress and anxiety because you are never behind.
- More opportunities and career growth.
- More time for leisure and recreation.

As an entrepreneur you need to apply time management by learning the following:

- How to do the (to do list).
- How to do the scheduling.
- And how to prioritize.

Let's start with the To Do List

Simply when we have our plan done, we can easily know what

we have every month from looking at the task table from our plan which looks like this as we discussed in the operational planning chapter:

The Task Table for the marketing department		
What (the means)	When	How much (the cost)
1- Promote the business on social media. 2-	January	$1000
1- Prepare a Facebook ad to generate 1000 lead. 2- Lunch a social media marketing campaign on Facebook to generate 1000 leads	1-5th of February 2-6th of February	1-$0 2-$1000
3- Promote new service on social media	1-2nd of March	1-$XXX
	April	
	May	
	June	
	July	
	August	
	September	
	October	
	November	
	December	
Total cost		Sum of all amounts

So, we have a table like the one above for departments and each department creates a table like the following, for its individuals:

The Task Table for Sam the operation manager		
What (the means)	When	How much (the cost)
1- 2- 3- 4-	January	5- $300 6- $0 7- $500 8- $700
1- 2-	February	
	March	
	April	
	May	
	June	
	July	
	August	
	September	
	October	
	November	
	December	
Total cost		Sum of all amounts

As we can see after we do the planning right, we will have a mechanical process that leads our organization to success in all aspects.

To Do List:

Each individual in the organization will take his task table and will take all the tasks of each month and put them in a daily to do list or in any organizer application (there are a lot of organizing software nowadays). It is so important to keep all your organizers and calendars synchronized on all of your devices.

Before we get to the to do list table, we need to discuss the scheduling and prioritizing first.

Scheduling:

We are going to divide each month into four weeks and we are going to divide our tasks on these four weeks according to the deadline of the task.

We know that some tasks may require several days or even months to be done so, what we are going to do is, scanning the task table from the plan and see what tasks may require more than one month to be done.

For example, we have an exhibition on March 15th and we know that to be prepared for this exhibition we need to start working on it a month and a half before so we take this task and put a note that starting date should be 45 days prior the deadline that means I need to put this task on January to start working on it.

In this way, we will know how to schedule our tasks throughout the year by knowing the tasks that need more time and require starting them earlier from the tasks that we can do within the same month.

Prioritizing:

While we are scanning our task table, we will start to put notes on the priorities of each task.

Sometimes employees or departments start to conduct activities that are really time wasters and they have nothing to do with achieving the goals of the organization.

How to prioritize tasks:

Tasks usually have four categories according to priority:

We need to identify the importance and the urgency of the task

1- **Important**: these tasks have an important role and outcome to our business goals, and other tasks depend on them to be done.
2- **Urgent**: these tasks demand immediate attention, and they are usually associated with achieving someone else's goals. They are often the ones we concentrate on and they demand attention because the consequences of not dealing with them are immediate.

Important and Urgent	Important but not urgent
Do it now	Schedule a time to do it
Not important but urgent	**Not important and not urgent**
Delegate or reschedule	Eliminate (delete)

Important and Urgent: If you have a lot of urgent and important activities, you should identify which of these activities or tasks you could have foreseen, and think about how you could schedule similar activities ahead of time so that they don't become urgent.

Important but not urgent: Make sure that you have plenty of time to do these tasks properly so that they do not become urgent.

Not important but urgent: These tasks prevent you from achieving your goals. Ask yourself whether you can reschedule or delegate them.

Not important and not urgent: these tasks are time wasters and some of them may be tasks that other people want you to do, even though they don't contribute to your own desired outcomes. Eliminate these tasks and try to say No to people who are trying to make you do their job for them.

Now let's take an example of how the (to do list) would be:

After we learned that scheduling is important to know when to start with the task and prioritizing the task according to the importance and urgency. We start to fill our to do list with the tasks have been assigned from the plan (the task table) then we start adding the day to day tasks according to priorities to our daily calendar.

We can use google, apple, or outlook calendar, or any other calendar you feel comfortable to use.

Don't forget to synchronize your calendar over your devices.

January To Do List				
What (the means)	Due date	priority	How much (the cost)	Notes
1- Task 1	1/07/2020	high	$250	
2- Task 2	1/10/2020	low	$1000	
3- Task 3	1/10/2020	Medium	$0	
4- Task 4	1/30/2020		$0	

Task analysis

How to do things more efficiently:

Efficiency: is defined as a level of performance that uses the lowest amount of inputs to create the greatest amount of outputs.

Task analysis:

To do tasks more efficiently we need to analyze the task with the following criteria by identifying:

- The Need.
- The personal suitability.
- The efficiency.

The need: ask the following question:

Does this task really need to be done?

Sometimes people spend a lot of time doing things that are not really necessary and they don't really need to be done.

The personal suitability: ask the following question:

Am I the right person to do this task?

Is someone else better suited or equipped to do this task?

Is it better to delegate this task and give it to a lower position to free your time to do bigger things?

Some kinds of tasks could prevent you or slow you down from focusing on the real goals and the big picture.

Try to delegate or outsource these kinds of tasks.

Efficiency: ask the following question:

Can this task be done in a better way?

Or is there a more efficient way to do this task?

Now let's see how this process will be.

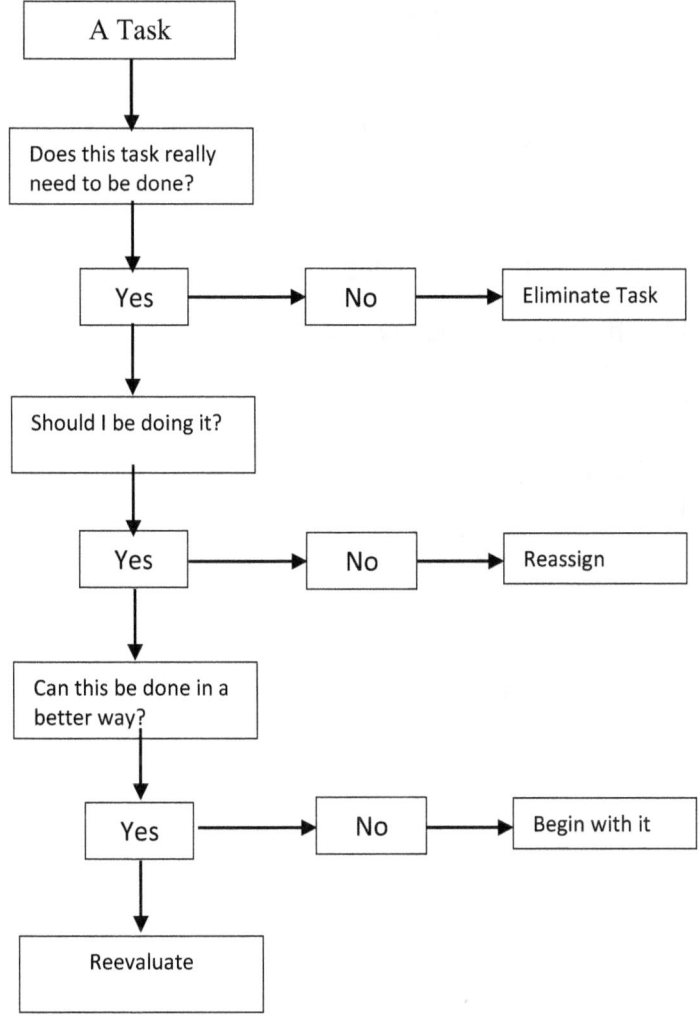

MODULE -3-

DIRECTING

Chapter 9: Introduction to Directing

Chapter 10: Effective Communication

Chapter 11: Motivation

Chapter 12: Leadership

CHAPTER 9

INTRODUCTION TO DIRECTING

INTRODUCTION TO DIRECTING

Directing is the process of guiding, instructing, counseling, overseeing, inspiring, motivating, and leading people towards achieving the desired predetermined goals of the organization. Directing is a continuous process that goes on throughout the life of the organization.

Directing will determine how to proceed with the business operations of the organization towards fulfilling the vision of that organization.

Let's take a look at some highlights on the importance of the managerial process of directing:

- Directing makes the organization goal-oriented
- It ensures that everybody in the organization rowing in the same direction.
- It initiates actions.
- It ensures efficient utilization of resources.
- It Ingrates Efforts
- It creates a motivated workforce.
- It ensures employee discipline.
- It ensures effective communication within the organization.
- It makes sure to keep the organization's operations on track as the plan, and many more,.

There are three major areas in directing that every entrepreneur should be good at:

- Effective communications.
- Motivation.

- Leadership.

We will discuss each of these areas in detail in the following three chapters.

So, let's start with the effective communications.

CHAPTER 10

EFFECTIVE COMMUNICATION

EFFECTIVE COMMUNICATION

What is communication?

Communication: is to convey and exchange information, ideas, or thoughts from one person to another, or from one end to the other.

Communication in business is very essential for the success of the organization.

As an entrepreneur, it is very important to understand and improve the communication skills and the business communication model to be a good manager and leader for your organization.

To be effective in communication and especially in business communication, you need to understand the elements of communication which basically form the business communication model.

Basic elements of communication:

The four basic elements of communication:

1- Encoder (sender).
2- Decoder (receiver).
3- A Message.
4- A communication channel.

Encoder/sender: is a person who has a message to convey or communicate.

Decoder/receiver: is the recipient of a message.

The responsibilities of the sender and receiver:

The main responsibility of the sender/encoder is:

To **encode** which means to:

1- convert the message or information into the best format for sending it to the receiver.
2- Ensure the intent of the message is conveyed and understood by the receiver.
3- Choosing the language, words, and graphical and other non-verbal forms of communication.

The main responsibility of the receiver/decoder is:

To **decode** which means to:

1- Determine the original intent of the sender.
2- Practices active listening in order to determine the intent of the message.
3- Provides feedback.

Encoding

- Encodes messages.
- Chooses the right channel.
- Chooses the right medium.
- Solicits feedback.
- Tries to minimize noise.

Decoding

- Decodes messages.
- Practices active listening.
- Provides feedback.

The Message:

Is the information that needs to be communicated or conveyed.

The message transforms from its raw form to its encoded form before it is being conveyed to the receiver.

The most important thing for the sender is to know the purpose of the message.

To have a clear purpose of the message you can ask the following questions:

- What are we trying to achieve by sending this message?
- Are we just trying to give information to the receiver?
- Are we trying to persuade or motivate?
- What do we want the recipient (receiver) to do?

Communication channel and medium:

We need to understand the difference between the channel and the medium to understand business communication.

Let's take the following example:

If we have some goods and we want to ship these goods from one place to another, the first thing we decide is whether we are going to ship the shipment by:

- Air.
- Ground.
- Sea.

These three options are our channels to ship this shipment, and let's say that we have decided to ship this shipment using the **ground** channel then we have to decide how:

- Truck.
- Car.
- Train.

These three options are the mediums.

So, Channel is the major way to communicate and the medium is the specific means used to communicate.

In communication we have two main channels:

- Verbal.
- Non-verbal.

In each one of these channels, we have the means to communicate which are the mediums.

In verbal we can divide this channel into two parts:

- Oral.
- Written.

In non-verbal we can divide this channel into:

- Kinesics (body language).
- Haptics (touch).
- Chronemics (time).
- Proxemics (personal space).

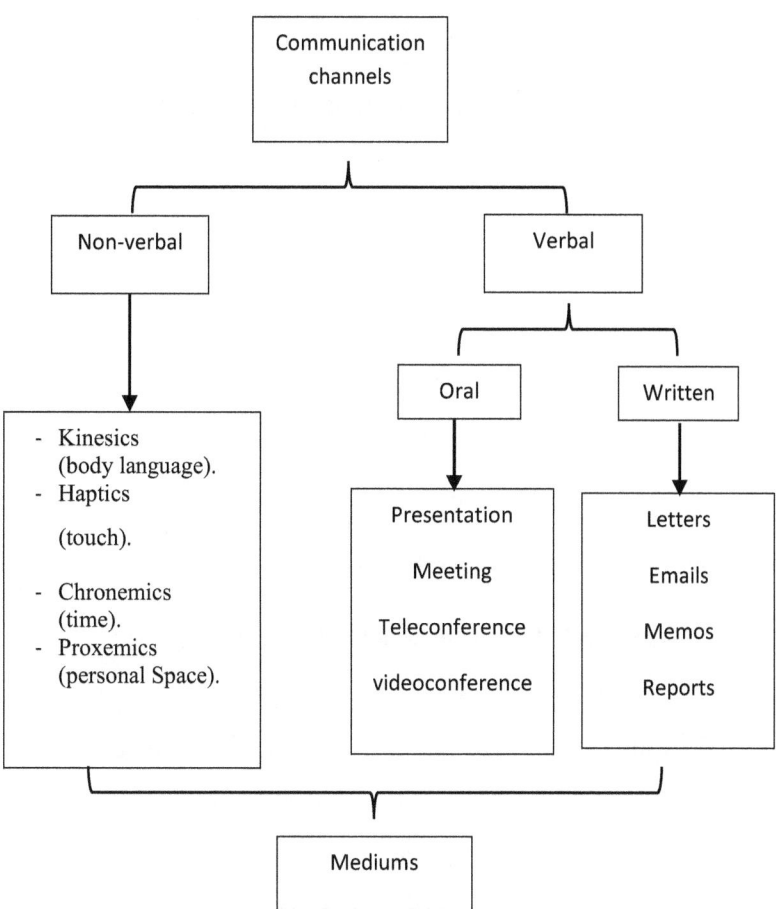

Communication barriers:

Here are some of the communication barriers that you as an entrepreneur should work to overcome.

- Message distraction.
- Noise.
- Poor communication skills.
- Poor listening skills.
- Differences in language comprehension.
- Information overload.

How to overcome these barriers.

- Message distraction: remember the main purpose is to get the receiver to understand your message, so try to avoid and eliminate any unnecessary elements from the message.
- Noise: Noise can be external and internal
    A- **External:** like you are having a meeting and there is construction noise in the street next to you, people will be distracted so reschedule the meeting or change the meeting place.
    B- **Internal:** like going to work and you have some serious family problems, that will affect your communication at work, so if you have a similar situation try to reschedule your important meetings if you feel that you can't focus.
- Poor communication skills: when you lack the communication skills that will affect your message and the

receiver may misunderstand the main purpose of your message.

- Poor listening skills: when there is a lack of listening skills the message will not be received or a big portion of the message will be lost, to avoid this try to practice active listening and try, if necessary, to take notes to help you comprehend the entire message.

- Differences in language comprehension: weakness in deferent language will lead to misunderstanding, so even learn the other language well or seek help from someone how is really good in that language to make sure your message has been delivered properly.

- Information overload: try not to overwhelm the receivers with too much information so they don't lose track always try to simplify the information and make sure to get the feedback that your message has been delivered.

Basics of communication:

Basic requirements of communication

In order to have an effective business communication you need to understand the basic requirements of communication when you focus on these requirements in all aspects of the communications of the organization then you can convey the message and achieve the purpose of it.

The basic requirements are:

    1- Defining the message

    2- Analyzing the audience.

    3- Structuring the message.

1- Defining the message

Every message has its purpose and the purpose of the message can be identified by determining the goals and objectives of that message.

Message goal: is the main aim and intent of the process of communication.

Message objective: is the method used to achieve the main goal of the message.

In business communication messages can be persuasive or informative. So, in order to **identify the goal of our message,** we should ask ourselves the following questions

What is the goal of my message?

What do I want the receiver to do?

To **identify the objectives of the message** we need to ask the following questions?

What are the methods that the receiver should follow in order to get to what I want him to do (to get to the goal of the message)?

What steps should be followed?

Once you answer these questions related to the goals and objectives of the message you have identified the purpose of the message.

Example:

Dear Mary

Greetings

Our customer decided to buy the house on Main street please prepare the contract before the meeting tomorrow at 9:00 AM. You can find all of his information with my secretary.

Thank you.

Regards.

Noor

[Message goal → points to "prepare the contract before the meeting"]

[Message objective → points to "You can find all of his information with my secretary"]

We can see the goal of the message is to *prepare the contract* but to prepare the contract we need *the information of the customer and the property and where to find this information,* these are the objectives of the message.

2- Analyzing the audience

To analyze the audience, it is good to ask the following questions:

1- Who makes up the audience?
2- What is the relationship that existed between ourselves and our audience?
3- What are the expectations of our audience?
4 What is the background of our audience? (cultural, social, religious, economic, and intellectual background).
5- What motivates our audience.

6- What is the timeframe that we can use to communicate with our audience without losing them (attention span)?

3- Structuring the message

Any message whether it was written, oral, or audiovisual should have the following element of structure:

1- Introduction.
2- Body.
3- Conclusion.

The introduction is the opening of our message and it should state the goal of our message and it usually represents 5% of our message.

The Body is where we clarify the goal or goals of our message, and where we clearly explain all the steps requires (the objectives needed) to achieve the goals of our message.

Organizing the objectives is very important, where you take the audience (the receiver) on a journey through the steps needed step by step to make them take the action you want which is the goal of the message.

The body of the message represents 88% -90% of the message.

It is good when you prepare the body of the message to address the following questions in the body of the message:

- What do you want the audience (receiver) to do?
- Why should it be done? (the goal of the message)

- How should it be done? (the objectives step by step)
- When does it need to be done?
- What are the supporters of my message? (stories, examples, testimonials, etc.)

The conclusion: is the summary of your message you should recap the action required and the benefits of taking that action if it was a persuasive message (sales message).

The conclusion represents 5% -7% of the entire message.

CHAPTER 11

MOTIVATION

MOTIVATION

What is motivation?

Motivation is the reason why you are doing something or the level of desire you have to do something.

So, a good definition of motivation is the ability to convince yourself or others to move towards achieving a specific goal.

Does motivation always work?

The answer is No.

- It's a very important rule to know: (When there is no desire, there is no motivation).

If someone has no desire at all of doing something no matter what you do, he or she will never do that thing.

- Another important rule to know: (The most powerful motivator is the belief).

When someone really believes in something, he or she will be self-motivated and needs no motivator to do what leads to his belief, as well as, no matter what you offer that person he or she will never be motivated to do anything against his belief because there is no desire.

For example:

When you look at most of the successful entrepreneurs or businessmen or businesswomen, like Steve Jobs, Bill Gates, Mark Zuckerberg, or Oprah Winfrey, you will find that they all share one thing, they all have a belief, and no matter what happened in their lives form difficulties, they were always self-motivated because they believed in something.

All of these names no matter what would you offer them or try to motivate them in any way to let go or abandon their belief they would never do that because they have no desire.

These are two rules in motivation in life, now let's take a look at motivation theories in management.

Motivation theories

How to motivate employees to make them work better, faster, and with less effort. This is a question every entrepreneur should have an answer to it.

Low motivation has a lot of bad consequences, as it leads to low engagement, poor performance, and, eventually, high turnover among employees.

Theoretical concepts of motivation provide different angles of explanations of how motivation works. The most exciting thing is, that motivation can be influenced and managed.

Most theories of motivation are used in management to improve individuals' and teams' work results

Let's see how these theories can be applied in your organization.

Maslow's Needs Hierarchy Theory

In 1943 Abraham Maslow a concept suggests that human needs are classified in a hierarchical system, ranging from physiological needs such as food and sleep, to self-actualization, and as soon as the lower-level need is satisfied, it no longer works as a motivator for the person. As long as lower-order needs are not satisfied, higher-order ones are not yet relevant.

And this is one of the most famous motivation theories that can be applied to any area of life.

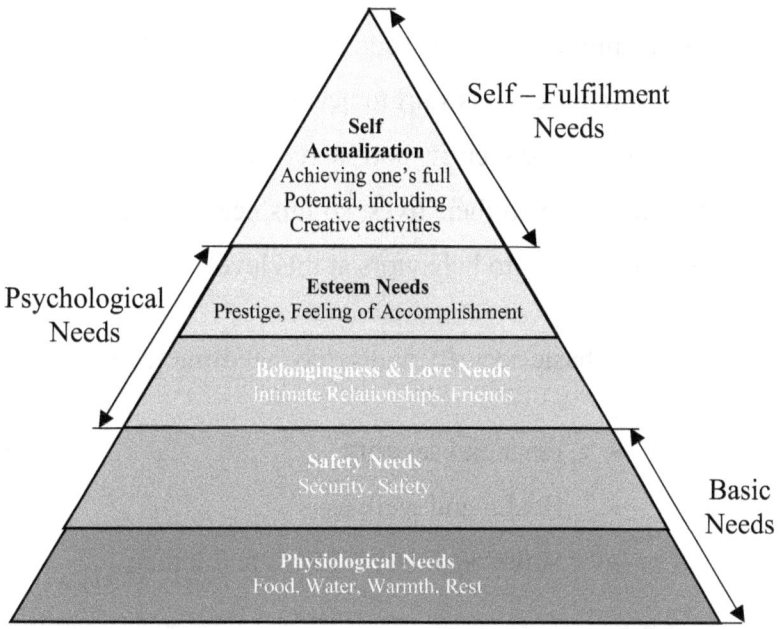

Maslow divided the needs of a person into 5 categories each one of these categories could be a motivation until it fulfilled, the motivation will move up to the next level in the hierarchy, and so on until a person achieves the self-actualization level.

Physiological Needs:

The basic physiological needs that are essential to survival.

- Food
- Water
- Breathing
- Shelter

Security and Safety Needs

As we move up to the second level of Maslow's hierarchy of needs, the requirements start to become a bit more complex. At this level, the needs for security and safety become primary. People want control and order in their lives, so this need for safety and security contributes largely to behaviors at this level.

Some of the basic security and safety needs include:

- Financial security
- Health and wellness
- Safety against accidents and injury

Finding a job, obtaining health insurance and health care, contributing money to a savings account, and moving into a safer neighborhood are all examples of actions motivated by the security and safety needs.

Together, the safety and physiological levels of the hierarchy make up what is often referred to as the basic needs.

Social Needs

The social needs in Maslow's hierarchy include such things as love, acceptance, and belonging. At this level, the need for emotional relationships drives human behavior. Some of the things that satisfy this need include:

- Friendships
- Romantic attachments
- Family
- Social groups
- Community groups
- Religious organizations

In order to avoid problems such as loneliness, depression, and anxiety, it is important for people to feel loved and accepted by other people. Personal relationships with friends, family, and lovers play an important role, as well as involvement in other groups that might include religious groups, sports teams, book clubs, and other group activities.

Esteem Needs

At the fourth level in Maslow's hierarchy is the need for appreciation and respect. When the needs at the bottom three levels have been satisfied, the esteem needs begin to play a more prominent role in motivating behavior.

At this point, it becomes more and more important to gain the respect and appreciation of others. People have a need to accomplish things and then have their efforts recognized.

In addition to the need for feelings of accomplishment and prestige, esteem needs include such things as self-esteem and personal worth. People need to sense that they are valued and by others and feel that they are making a contribution to the world. Participation in professional activities, academic accomplishments, athletic or team participation, and personal hobbies can all play a role in fulfilling the esteem needs.

People who are able to satisfy the esteem needs by achieving good self-esteem and the recognition of others tend to feel confident in their abilities. Those who lack self-esteem and the respect of others can develop feelings of inferiority.

Together, the esteem and social levels make up what is known as the psychological needs of the hierarchy.

Self-Actualization Needs

At the very peak of Maslow's hierarchy are the self-actualization needs. "What a man can be, he must be," Maslow explained, referring to the need people have to achieve their full potential as human beings.

According to Maslow's definition of self-actualization:

"It may be loosely described as the full use and exploitation of talents, capabilities, potentialities, etc. Such people seem to be fulfilling themselves and to be doing the best that they are capable of doing... They are people who have developed or are developing to the full stature of which they capable."

Self-actualizing people are self-aware, concerned with personal growth, less concerned with the opinions of others, and interested in fulfilling their potential.

Why to apply this?

Many entrepreneurs are still not taking the upper level of the pyramid (Self-Actualization Needs) into account. They are more focused on the lower levels – which is not bad, as it results in creating high income and job security. But for sure when you achieve the self-actualization level in your organization that would drive better results. One of the best results, when you apply the (Self-Actualization Needs), is that you would have high professional employees who are loyal and have no need to leave your organization to look for a better chance.

Frederick Herzberg's Motivator-Hygiene (Two-Factor) Theory

In this theory there are two groups of factors, first group of factors (motivation factors) are intrinsic to the workplace and increase employees' levels of satisfaction and motivation while the second group (hygiene factors) are the factors that cause dissatisfaction, all of which act independently of each other.

Motivators:

- The following are examples of the first group and work as motivators: (recognition for one's achievement, opportunity to do something meaningful, challenging work, responsibility, involvement in decision making, sense of importance to an organization, etc.) All of these factors lead to employee satisfaction, coming from intrinsic conditions of the job like personal growth, recognition, and achievement.

Hygiene factors:

- The following are examples of the second group that works as hygiene factors: (salary, benefits, status, job security, work conditions, benefits, vacations, paid insurance, etc.) where the absence of these factors does not lead to a positive satisfaction and motivation. The term "hygiene" is used with these factors because Herzberg considers them as maintenance factors. they are extrinsic to the work itself and include many aspects such as company policies and procedures, salaries, supervisory and management practices, and interpersonal relationships at work, etc.

How to apply this?

Just try to reduce the factors that lead to dissatisfaction and work on increasing and strengthening the factors that lead to satisfaction

Take a look at the following chart and try always to position your organization as an entrepreneur in the upper right corner of the chart.

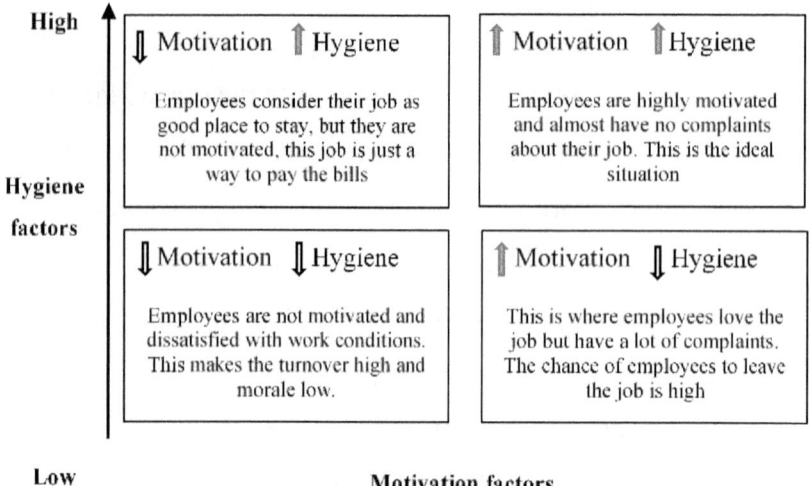

Douglas McGregor's Participation Theory

McGregor's Participation Theory is also known as Theory X and Theory Y which describes two approaches to people's attitudes towards work.

In theory X we find that workers or employees have little to no ambition, and they tend to avoid responsibility and are focused on their individual goals. We find that managers in this theory, are focused on: overcoming their employees' laziness and pursuit of their self-interest by applying closer supervision, disciplinary measures, and using micromanagement overall work aspects, and they tend to use direct rewards for desired behavior.

In theory Y we consider employees are motivated towards achieving team goals, and enjoy what they do at their job, and they don't need direct rewards or punishments in order to do a better job.

In theory Y, managers are more focused on shaping their teams and delivering team goals to their employees, building healthy relationships among employees at the workplace, emphasizing the sense of responsibility, and granting more authorities to them.

In the picture below you can see how workers in Theory X refuse to take on work and responsibility, In Theory Y workers welcome it.

How to apply this?

You should look at these two theories as two separate concepts so the best practice for managers is to combine both theories according to their employees' personality, workplace conditions, and organization regulation, policies, and procedures, etc.

Having employees like the ones in theory Y is something great but unfortunately, the case is not like this most of the times, so you need to work on the employees that are categorized under Theory X to encourage them and take them to the next level as the ones in Theory Y, and if they are not willing to change sometime getting rid of this type of employees is way better.

David McClelland's Need Theory

In the 1960s McClelland developed his theory where he points out that regardless of age, sex, race, or culture, all of us possess one of these needs and are driven by it.

In this motivational theory, we find that the needs for achievement, power, and affiliation, influence the behavior of individuals significantly.

Opposed to Maslow's needs hierarchy theory, this theory identifies motivators as separate, non-hierarchical needs:

1- The need for achievement.
2- The need for power.
3- The need for affiliation.

Need for achievement (n Ach) defines employees' motivation to excel, to do better work, and to compete with the standard of excellence. Individuals who are motivated by the need for achievement usually have a strong desire of setting up difficult goals and objectives and accomplishing them to get to the satisfaction level that they are looking for. They prefer to work in a results-oriented work environment and they always appreciate any feedback on their work. individuals in this category calculate risks to reach their goals and they tend to avoid both high-risk situations (so they don't fail) and low-risk situations (it is so easy for them).

Need for power (n Pow) is the need to have an impact on others, to change people, and to make a difference. Individuals who are motivated by the need for power have a desire to control and influence others. Competition motivates them and they enjoy winning arguments. Having status and recognition is something they aspire for, and they do not like to be on the losing side at all.

The need for affiliation (n Aff) is the desire to establish friendly relationships with people around. Individuals who are motivated by the need for affiliation Always prefer being part of a group. They spend a lot of their time socializing and maintaining relationships and they have a strong desire to be loved and accepted. These types of people are always afraid of being rejected.

How to apply this?

Identifying the needs of your employees and match their needs with the roles that you are going to assigning to them accordingly. When you choose the right roles for each one of them helps to increase their motivation.

For example:

1- Managerial positions perfectly fit individuals who have the need for power because it triggers their motivations.

2- Jobs with analytical positions fit individuals who are motivated by the need for achievement.

3- Positions where communication and soft skills are needed perfectly fit individuals who have the need for affiliation.

Job Characteristics Theory

Greg Oldham and Richard Hackman, have developed this theory as a theory of work design, that focuses on job enrichment.

This theory represents a model of five key job characteristics that influence motivation, satisfaction, and performance:

1- **Skill variety:** the characteristic of this job responsibilities requires mastering skills and developing talents. Which adds personal interest to this kind of job by involving self-development and actualization.

2- **Task identity:** the characteristic of this job gives the ability to perform a task and achieve a visible outcome. This means that employees are being involved in the entire work process and they can see the importance of their work for the team's result and outcome.

3- **Task significance:** the characteristic of this job has an effect on other people's lives. By being able to improve other people's well-being makes a job significantly meaningful.

4- **Autonomy:** the characteristic of this job is giving freedom and independency to the employees to perform their duties. It ensures the ability to achieve self-actualization through applying their own efforts, initiatives, and decisions to the work process.

5- **Feedback:** the characteristic of this job is to give the ability to the employee to know the results of his or her one work and be aware of how its outcome is perceived and evaluated. Providing clear information on the employees' work results increases their ability to improve performance, technique, or workflow to achieve better outcomes.

How to apply this at the workplace?

By analyzing the character of the employees and giving them the job that fits their characters, would make them realizes the impact of their work on other team members, customers, and know the impact of their actions on the process of the work and the outcome, that would increase employees' motivation, reduces turnover and improves teamwork.

After learning all of these approaches and theories of motivation, as an entrepreneur director, you need to have a balance between theories and real life, the smart director will learn all of these theories and know where and when to apply each one of them or create a mix of them to be suitable to his or her organization's situation.

CHAPTER 12

LEADERSHIP

LEADERSHIP

The definition of leadership:

Leadership in simple words: is a process where a person influences another person or a group of people towards achieving a specific goal or goals.

As we can see, there are **two main factors** in the process of leadership:

One: to have a **leader** who influences others.

Two: to have **followers** influenced by that leader to achieve the desired goal.

The definition of a leader:

A leader is a person who is responsible for leading followers to achieve a goal or a vision.

The definition of a follower:

A follower is a person who subordinates to the influence, directions, and guidance of a leader.

Leaders motivate, inspire, direct, and empower their followers in order to become effective leaders.

The characteristics of an effective leader:

Effective leaders usually have most of these characteristics and features that distinguish them from other people.

The effective leader should have:

Justice: the ability to do right and to be impartial in judgment.

Judgment: has the ability to weigh facts, and come up with solutions and alternatives for whatever situations he faces.

Integrity: to be honest and truthful.

Initiative: the ability to take actions without even having an order.

Decisiveness: the ability to make decisions quickly and effectively.

Dependability: the quality of being trustworthy and reliable.

Endurance: the ability to endure an unpleasant or difficult process or situation without giving up.

Tact or diplomacy: cleverness in dealing with others or with difficult issues.

Courage: the ability to be fearless, calm, and firm when facing difficulties.

Enthusiasm: having an intense interest and enjoyment in what needs to be achieved.

Knowledge: to know your job well, your team, and yourself.

Unselfishness: the quality of not putting yourself first but being willing to put others ahead of self.

Loyalty: the quality of being loyal to someone or something, in this case to your team and your organization.

Skills that leaders should develop:

- Planning.
- Coaching.
- Team building.
- Decision making.
- Communicating.

- Flexibility.
- Risk-taking.
- Facilitating.
- Motivating.

The responsibilities of the leader:

- **Developing a vision:** as we learned earlier on how to develop a vision, leaders know exactly and clearly where they want to be, and it is their responsibility to communicate the vision of the organization to their team and make sure that everyone is rowing in the same direction.
- **Developing a mission and goals:** We have learned earlier in this book how to develop the mission statement and set the goals of the organization. After the vision is developed and you know where you are heading, the question is (how do you get there?). this where the mission is used to determine the goals needed to achieve the vision. It is the responsibility of the leader to develop the mission and the goals and make sure that they are very clear for the team members.
- **Working towards achieving goals:** achieving goals is what turns the vision of the organization into reality, this is why leaders should be goal-oriented to accomplish these goals.
- **Building a cohesive team:** teams within organizations are the units which are responsible for accomplishing goals and make them a reality, so it is the responsibility of leaders to build cohesive teams and make sure that communication among team members as well as the roles of each team member are clear and understood,
- **Coaching team members:** It is the responsibility of the leaders to direct their teams and coach them by providing

them with the required knowledge, information, and training to develop their skills and make them experts in what they do.
- **Identifying and meeting the team needs:** leaders are responsible for finding out what are the needs of their teams and provide them with the proper resource from information, tools, fund, and so on and make sure that they met their team needs to get the desired results.
- **Measuring team performance:** if you can't measure it you can't manage it, we know to achieve goals they should be measurable and as a leader, you need to measure the performance of the team because some people in your team might excel, while others might not perform well, so this is why leaders should set expectations and make sure they are clear to everyone so they can measure the performance of their team.
- **Holding team members accountable:** when leaders set the expectations of their teams, they should hold their team members accountable for not meeting the expectations or goals, and at the same time, leaders should recognize and reward members who have done exceptional work.
- **Motivating team members:** when leaders motivate their teams or employees that ignites creativity and gets the job done with excellent results and good vibes among the team.

Differences between managers and leaders:

Managers	Leaders
Managers focus on controlling resources.	Leaders focus on empowering people
Managers focus on structure.	Leaders focus on people.
Managers manage people as employees.	Leaders see people as part of a team.
Managers focus on the day to day tasks.	Leaders focus on fulfilling a vision.
Managers have a short-range perspective.	leaders have a long range perspective.
Managers focus on having work done.	Leaders create new opportunities to grow the business.
Not all mangers can lead	All effective leaders can manage

Leadership styles:

Leadership focuses mainly on two types of support, the relational and the functional support. Good leaders should know how to adapt according to the situation they are facing and should know where to provide more relational support and where to provide more functional support. That being said now we can understand how leadership has been divided into four major styles.

Relational support:

This type of support is people-oriented and focuses on the needs of the team and provides psychological support like appreciation, encouragement, and facilitation.

Functional support:

This type of support is task-oriented and focuses on supporting the team with things related to the needs of the business on the functional level where leaders provide guidance to accomplish business tasks.

The four main styles of leadership:

Directing:

In this style leaders determine the course of action needed to accomplish a certain task or goal by providing clear instructions and supervise the work process to get the desired results.

This implies that we are dealing with a high motivated – low experienced team, so this is why the leader in this style focuses more on the functional side of the support because the team does not need much focusing on the relational side (the team is already high-motivated).

Directing Style		
Leaders:	High Functional	Low relational
Team:	Low experience	High motivation

Selling:

In this style, leaders determine the course of action needed to accomplish a certain task or goal by providing clear instructions and supervise the work process to get the desired results. leaders also give a clear explanation and reasoning for this course of action as if they are selling their idea and decision to their followers and persuade the team towards their decision.

This implies that the team we are dealing with has low motivation and low experience.

Selling Style		
Leaders support:	High Functional	High relational
Team:	Low experience	Low motivation

Participating:

In this style, leaders act as facilitators where they focus more on the relational side of the support and provide encouragement and work on developing the relationship among the team members and raise the confidence in their abilities. Leaders in this style have less focus on the functional side of the support and do not play a major role on this level they only advice and facilitate.

This implies that we are dealing with a team that has high experience but has low motivation.

Participating Style		
Leaders support:	Low Functional	High relational
Team:	High experience	Low motivation

Delegation:

In this style, leaders give little support on both sides of functional and relational support and play the role of the advisor and facilitator, that's because they are dealing with a highly experienced and highly motivated team.

Delegation Style		
Leaders support:	Low Functional	Low relational
Team:	High experience	High motivation

Now let's take a look at the followers' side of the equation.

Types of Followers:

As we know leadership consist of two parts leaders, and followers.

Followers are individuals who follow the directions and guidance of a leader.

We also have four main types of follower:

Committed Novice:

In this type, the follower does not have enough knowledge,

experience, and capability to perform tasks, but the follower in this case is highly motivated.

An example of this type of follower is the newly graduated individuals who are usually very motivated to do the job but they lack experience, in this case, the leader should provide more functional support and less relational support.

Committed Novice Type		
Follower	Low experience	High motivation
Leadership style for this follower	Directing Style	

Uncommitted Expert:

In this type, followers have the knowledge, experience, and capability to perform tasks, but they have low motivation to do the job.

Leaders deal with this type of follower by focusing more on the relational support and pay very little attention to the functional support since the followers are expert individuals and they know how to perform the tasks assigned to them.

Uncommitted Expert Type		
Follower	High experience	Low motivation
Leadership style for this follower	Participating Style	

Committed Expert:

In this type, followers have the knowledge, experience, and capability to perform tasks, and they are also highly motivated to do the job.

This is the perfect type of followers, and every leader should work on his team to get them to this level where the team members are highly experts and highly motivated.

Committed Expert Type		
Follower	High experience	High motivation
Leadership style for this follower	Delegation Style	

Uncommitted Novice:

In this type, followers do not have the knowledge, experience, and capability to perform tasks, and they do not have the motivation to do the job as well.

Leaders have to put a lot of effort into both types of support functional and relational.

Uncommitted Novice Type		
Follower	Low experience	Low motivation
Leadership style for this follower	Selling Style	

MODULE -4-

CONTROLLING

Chapter 13: Introduction to Controlling.

Chapter 14: Setting Performance Standards.

Chapter 15: Measuring performance and types of Controls

Chapter 16: Adjusting

CHAPTER 13

INTRODUCTION TO CONTROLLING

INTRODUCTION TO CONTROLLING

To make an organization successful you need to make sure that you are performing the operation of controlling the right way. After finalizing the plans of an organization management needs to execute a series of steps to ensure that the plans are being executed as intended.

You can apply these steps almost to any plan for any department or project.

The steps of the controlling function:

1. Setting performance standards:

Good entrepreneurs should transform their plans into performance standards.

These performance standards can be in the form of goals or Key Performance Indicator KPI's as we have learned before,

2. Measuring actual performance:

Remember if you cannot measure it you cannot manage it. You need to measure the actual performance to be able to see if your standards are met or not.

3. Comparing actual performance with standards or goals:

After comparing the results of the actual performance with your standards you can accept or reject the outcome of the performance.

4. Analyzing deviations:

In case the standards have not been met, management should analyze why they haven't been met and try to find a solution to meet the standards. Remember that standards should be Specific,

Measurable, Agreed upon, and Realistic. In this step, we also can determine whether more control is necessary or if the standard should be changed.

5. Taking corrective action:

After analyzing the deviation and determining why the standards haven't been met, management can then develop solutions for those issues to meet the standards and make changes to processes or behaviors to get the desired results.

CHAPTER 14

SETTING PERFORMANCE STANDARDS

SETTING PERFORMANCE STANDARDS

1 - Setting Control/Performance Standards

Standards are the criteria that enable the management to evaluate future, current, or past actions.

Critical Success Indicators

In the world of management, we have many indicators and factors to measure the performance of the organizations and we call them critical success indicators

The most popular one is KPI Key Performance Indicator, most of the organizations use the KPI's to measure and keep tracking the performance according to their plan, and this is what we are going to focus on.

The definition of Key Performance Indicator, or KPI:

A KPI is an indicator that specifies the minimum acceptable amount of achievement for a certain goal.

KPI is a measure of performance within an organization, to evaluate the success of the business according to its primary objectives or strategic plan. KPIs vary widely, depending on the type of business and its goals.

KPIs are the measurable means of the leadership of any organization to evaluate the progress toward its short and long-term goals. We can set KPIs for a short period of time and KPIs for the whole period of the plan.

It is recommended that every SBU to have at least 3 KPI and no more than 10 KPI's so it could be realistic.

Let's take an example to understand KPI better:

An X car dealership sets a KPI of selling 12000 cars in the next coming 5 years.

That means selling 12000 cars is the minimum acceptable amount of sales that this dealership must achieve in 5 years, so let's say that after 5 years this dealership sold 15000 cars, that would be great because they exceeded their minimum goal of 12000 cars, but if they sold less than 12000 car that means that the management is not good and an action should be taken.

This is why we set short term KPIs so we can measure in the short run and adjust to avoid getting behind our desired goal on the period of our plan.

For the same example this dealership must sell 12000 cars in 5 years in this case we set a KPI for this year where we divide the 12000 / 5 = 2400 unit or car, in this case, we can measure the performance in one year to do any necessary action in case we could not achieve the minimum goal (KPI) of this year so we can adjust our plan accordingly.

Of course, this is just a simple example to understand the idea, this is why we divided the targeted sales number into 5 years, but what really happens is every year our sales should be increasing and every year we should have a growth over the year before.

We can have many Key performance indicators in any of the following perspectives according to our organization type:

- Finance perspective.
- Customer perspective.
- Operation perspective.
- Sales perspective.
- Marketing perspective.

- Environment perspective.
- Information technology perspective.

We can say for example:

- We want our client's number to be 500 clients (client KPI is 500 Clients).
- Our order fulfillment is no more than 1 hour.
- Our revenue per employee is $X amount of money.
- Our cost of lead is no more than $X amount of money.

CHAPTER 15

MEASURING PERFORMANCE AND TYPES OF CONTROLS

Measuring performance and types of Controls

After we understood the importance of controlling function of the management process and we learned its step.

Let's take a look at the types of controls.

Computerized Control Systems:

Using computer software and hardware systems is one of the most effective tools of management to control the use of resources and ensure to have the desired efficiency and productivity within the organization.

Utilizing the right system and technology and implementing them to the business process can provide the management with measurements and control that can help to prevent the misuse of resources and ensure that the business process is going as intended to be.

Let's take a look at the type of these systems:

1- **Loop system:** an example of this system is accounting software that can track all transactions like purchases and payments of ordered items. This type of system can provide measurements of control by identifying where the unexpected results have occurred, this will help the management to find out the mistakes that happened in the business process and reveal any violations that might happen in the organization's policies and procedures.
2- **Feedback System**: is a process to evaluate how effectively the goals have been met at the end of the production process.

The feedback system evaluates the team's progress by comparing the output that was planned to be achieved in the plan to the actual output. If what is produced actually is less than what was planned to, management can adjust the process to increase productivity to meet the plan. the feedback system is also used as a closed system where one process output is the input of another process within the organization, in this case, the feedback system determines efficiently the right amount of resources needed in a timely manner to supply the needed resources to a process that other processes in the organization depend on to start.

An example of this system is computer software that is able to control and track the fulfillment process and calculate the amount of the raw materials needed to be purchased in a timely fashion to meet the future orders.

3- **Automatic Control:** this type of systems is used in business processes where fault tolerance or safety is extremely important, and we find that in the aviation industry where we find what we call (Autopilot) this type of hardware and software programing has automatic corrections to correct errors before they happen to minimize the risk.

4- **Feed Forward Systems:** this type of systems is used mostly in the manufacturing processes, the computer software forecasts errors in the output by conducting a constant analysis for the process and quickly correct or signal the changes needed to be done on the input.

Quantitative Measures of Control

Quantitative measurement is the measurement of data that can be translated into numbers. Data has to be in numerical form because the goal of quantitative measurement is to run statistical analysis.

There have been a lot of established measuring systems that have been adopted and implemented over decades across the business world that can help us to measure and monitor our business. Let's take a look at some common systems and techniques for measuring that are being used in controlling function.

Production Environment controls

Gantt Charts

Gantt chart is a visual view of tasks scheduled over time. Gantt charts are used for planning projects of all sizes and they are very useful to show what work and tasks are scheduled to be done on a specific day. They also help you view the start and end dates of a project in one simple view.

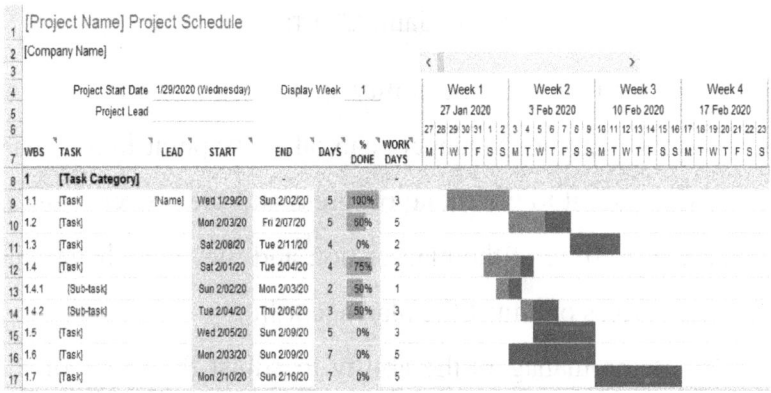

These charts are usually developed during the planning and scheduling phase of the business. The charts allow us to visualize all the processes and tasks of the entire project, so we can look at the entire plan of the business or the project with an eagle's eye view. This helps with identifying where are we now and what tasks need to be done and which tasks are dependent on other tasks.

Gantt Chart helps the managers to do the following:

- Make a realistic analysis of the success and the closing of the business projects.
- Maintaining the order of the activities need to be done according to the priorities, to achieve the desired goals.
- Having a visual image of the dependencies of the tasks to know which task in the business process depending on what.
- Knowing the resources needed at all times and places along the process of the work.

When we have the Gantt Chart done, we can compare our actual progress with what was planned by looking at the chart and see if we are on the right track.

We have two major benefits of Gantt Chart:

1- It gives the managers the ability to know how the progress of the work is going. Managers can take any point in the chart and compare it to the actual progress and see if everything is going according to the plan or not, and they can change the work process or adjust the plan accordingly.
2- It gives the managers the ability to adjust the speed of the work to meet the deadlines. That can be done with the tasks

that haven't started yet and based on the current situation where managers can do adjustments and maybe provide more resources, or assign more qualified employees, or more funds for certain tasks to meet the deadlines and achieve the desired goals.

Program Evaluation and Review Technique (PERT).

PERT is an acronym that stands for **P**rogram **E**valuation and **R**eview **T**echnique. It is a model for managing business projects or processes as it analyzes and represents the project's tasks.

PERT chart is used to find out how much time will be required to finish each task in the project. This leads to figuring out the minimum time needed to complete the whole project.

PERT is a tool that the planning department and management use to cater to uncertainty by making it possible to do the scheduling for a project even without knowing the exact details and timeframe of all tasks in the project.

With this method, you don't have to start your plan with a beginning and an end because this method is focused on making events happen rather than focusing on the start and completion of a project, and since it's focused on events, you can create one without knowing every detail.

PERT is used more with projects that the timeline is more important than the cost, like research and development projects.

PERT has three-time estimates to calculate the **Expected Time Value:**

(Tm)- Time Mostly - The Most Likely Time Estimate: This represents the most probable amount of time to complete the task or project. In other words, it is the best estimate of how long it will take to accomplish the task or activity, assuming there are no problems.

(To) – Time Optimistic – The Optimistic Time Estimate: which represents the optimistic or shortest time, or the least amount of time to accomplish a task or activity. This is a scenario when everything is working well and you beat the estimated schedule.

(Tp) – Time Pessimistic – The Pessimistic Time Estimate:

Which represents the pessimistic or longest time, the maximum amount of time to accomplish a task or activity. This is the worst-case scenario.

(Te) – The Expected Time Value:

The expected value = [Optimistic + Pessimistic +(4*Most likely)]/6

$$Te = \frac{To + 4Tm + Tp}{6}$$

$$\text{Standard Deviation} = \frac{Tp - To}{6}$$

General rule:

- The task or project will be completed with the range of Te ± 1 the standard deviation is 68.26% of the time.
- The task or project will be completed with the range of Te ± 2 the standard deviation is 95.44% of the time.
- The task or project will be completed with the range of Te ± 3 the standard deviation is 99.73% of the time.

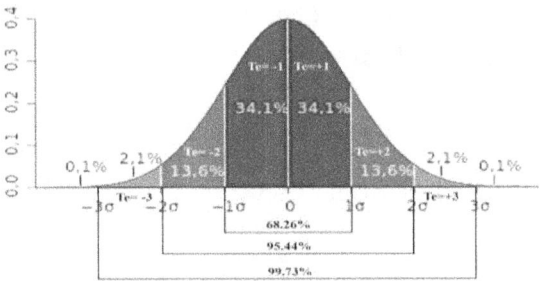

Standard deviation diagram Shows Te ± 1, Te ± 2 & Te ± 3

PERT chart us a tool that allows managers to make decisions about a project and adjust and make new decisions about the project at any time.

So how to create a PERT chart?

We have 3 rules to create a PERT chart:

1- Tasks (Activities) are represented as **Arrows**. ⟶
2- Milestone dates are represented as **Nodes**. ◯

3- Each activity or task should have a starting node and ending node and we connect them with an arrow that represents the activity or the task.

So, to construct the project network or create the PERT chart we need to know the predecessor for each task in other words, we need to know how the tasks are related to each other, what task depends on what task to start.

Let's take an example.

We have 10 activities for A to J and we have the predecessors for each activity and we have the (To, Tm, and Tp) Time Optimistic, Time Mostly, and Time Pessimistic.

Activity	predecessors	Duration (weeks)		
		O (optimistic)	M (Mostly)	P (pessimistic)
A	-	4	5	6
B	-	1	3	5
C	-	2	4	6
D	A	1	2	3
E	B	1	2	9
F	C	3	4	5
G	C	2	2	8
H	E, F	4	4	10
I	D	2	5	8
J	H, G	2	2	8

Now let's start constructing the project network.

When we look at the activities or tasks A, B, C, we have no

Predecessors for these activities, so we start with activity A and we draw a starting node and an ending node for it and we connect both nodes with an arrow:

In the diagram below we see that tasks A, B, and C started at node 1 since they have no predecessors' tasks.

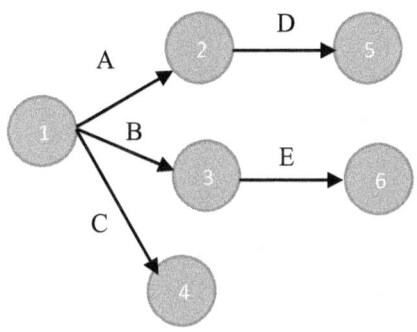

A started at node 1 and ended at node 2

B started at node 1 and ended at node 3

C started at node 1 and ended at node 4

Buy going back to the table of the example we find that

D started after its predecessor task A so D started where A ended.

D started at node 2 and ended at node 5

E started after its predecessor task B so E started where B ended.

D started at node 3 and ended at node 6

Now let's take a look at task F

F started after its predecessor task C so F started where C ended.

F started at node 4 but ended at node 6 because according to the table in the predecessor field, we find that task E and F end together so they both end at node 6.

Now, F started at node 4 and ended at node 6. Look at the diagram below:

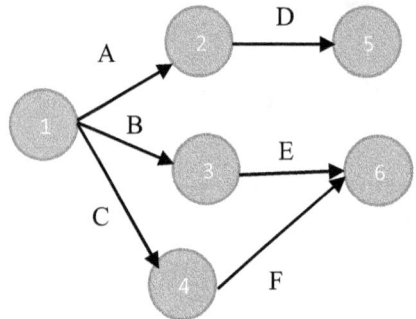

Now we have task or activity G

G started after its predecessor task C so G started where C ended.

G started at node 4 and ended at node 7

Look at the diagram on the next page:

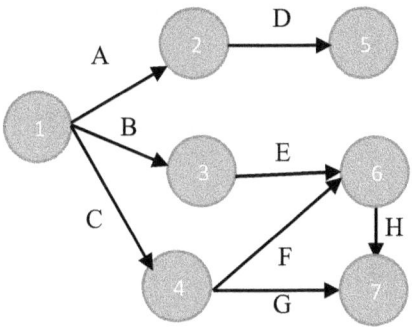

Now we have task H

H started at node 6 because H started after E and F ended but ended at node 7 because according to the table in the predecessor field, we find that task H and G end together so they both end at node 7.

So, H started at node 6 and ended at node 7

Now let's see task I:

I started after its predecessor task D so I started where D ended.

I started at node 5 and ended at node 8

Look at the diagram below

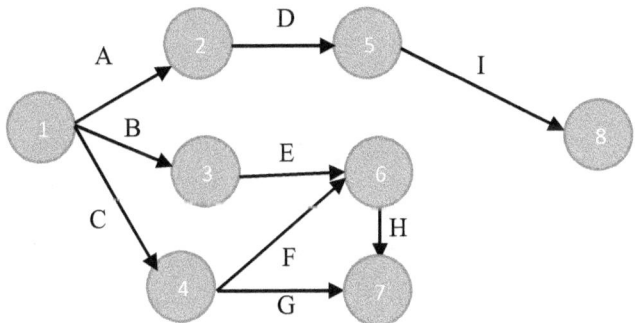

Now we have our last task or activity in the project which is J.

According to the table, J started after its predecessors' task H & G so J started where H & G ended.

I started at node 7 and ended at node 8 and this is the end of the project.

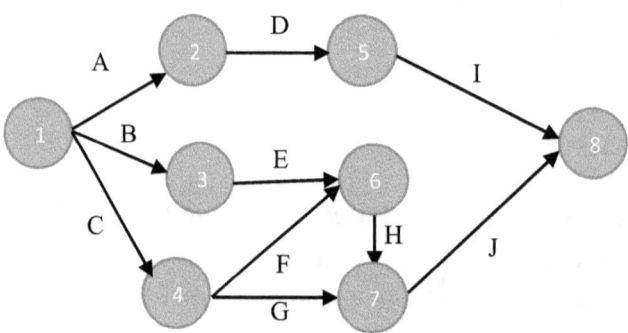

Now let's calculate the **Te** -The expected time value:

As we learned before

The expected value = [Optimistic + Pessimistic +(4*Most likely)]/6

$$Te = \frac{To + 4Tm + Tp}{6}$$

So, if we do the calculation, we will get the following table, these numbers show how many weeks is the duration of each task:

task	predecessors	To (optimistic)	Tm (Mostly)	Tp (pessimistic)	Te Expected
A	-	4	5	6	5
B	-	1	3	5	3
C	-	2	4	6	4
D	A	1	2	3	2
E	B	1	2	9	3
F	C	3	4	5	4
G	C	2	2	8	3
H	E, F	4	4	10	5
I	D	2	5	8	5
J	H, G	2	2	8	3

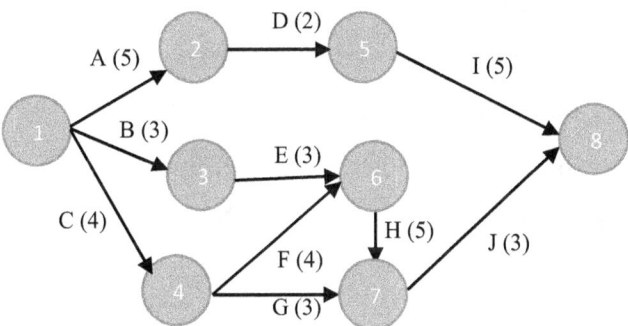

This is how we structure the project network and draw a PERT chart and point out what is the expected time for each task and what is the sequence of the tasks.

Critical Path Method (CPM)

Critical Path Method is a powerful tool and simple technique for planning, analyzing, and scheduling large, complex projects.

It is a very important tool to control tasks and resources of the project.

CPM is commonly used in research, development, engineering, and construction projects.

This method is very useful for the scheduling process of projects that have independent tasks.

Benefits of using CPM:

- Identifying all tasks needed to complete the project.
- Identifying the duration time for each task.
- Identifying the independencies or the connection among the tasks of the project.
- Determining the estimate of time duration for each task to be completed in a project.
- Determining which tasks that comprise a project, are critical in their effect on the project time to complete it.
- Providing a guide to prioritize tasks and ensuring timely project completion.

In this method CPM, we can label tasks as:

- Critical.
- Sub-critical.
- Non-critical.

To understand this method more let's take an example:

We have the following project and we can see the sequence of the tasks and we have the duration of the tasks given by days.

Task	Predecessors	Duration (days)
A	–	5
B	–	3
C	A, B	4
D	A, B	2
E	B	3
F	C	4
G	D	3
H	F, G	5
I	F, G	5
J	E, H	3

- First, we need to construct the project network as we did in the example of the PERT Chart example.
- To find out the critical path we need to do some calculations, we need to calculate the Earliest Start time ES and calculate the latest completion time LC for each node.

Each task will have two nodes, the starting node, and the ending node

We start with activity A and we draw a starting node and an ending node for it and we connect both nodes with an arrow:

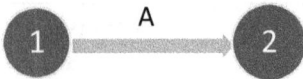

Above each node, we draw a rectangle divided into 2 boxes

The upper box is the Latest Completion Time and the lower box is the Earliest Start time.

| 1 | ⇨ Latest Completion Time |
| 2 | ⇨ Earliest Start time |

Latest Completion Time:

Rules:

- Latest Completion Time for the last node in the project is always equal to the Earliest Start time of the last node.
- We always go backward from the last node to the first node in the project to calculate the LS of the tasks.
- Going backward we start with nodes that have one arrow first then go to the nodes that have two or more arrows.
- When we have a node that is connected to two arrows, that means to get to this node, we have two tasks needs to be done, and we always take the **minimum time** of these two tasks to calculate the Latest Completion Time of that node which is connected to these two tasks.

Formula:

Latest completion time for a task = latest completion time for the task after that one minus the Duration of that task (which we are looking to calculate its latest completion time).

LCA = LCB-DA

As in the example below:

(LC) Latest Completion Time for the first node of task A= latest Completion time of the following task (node 2) – Duration of task A.

In case we have two tasks connected to this node we always take the minimum time of the two options.

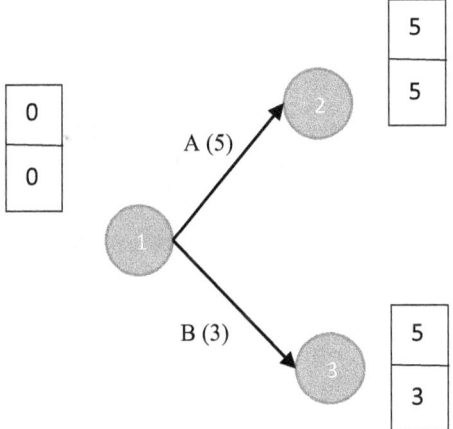

In the diagram above node 1 is connected to two nodes 2 and 3, to calculate the **(LC)** Latest Completion Time for node 1 we calculate the formula for both and choose the minimum time of both to put it in the box of the LC of the first node LC box.

The duration of task A is 5 days.

The duration of task B is 3 days.

Latest Completion Time for node 2 is 5 minus the duration of task A which is 5 = 0.

Latest Completion Time for node 3 is 5 minus the duration of task B which is 3 = 2.

So, we choose the first option which is 0 because it is the minimum time of the two options and we put it in the LC box of the first node as we can see in the diagram above.

Earliest Start time

Rules:

- The Earliest Start time for the first node is always 0 because we haven't started the project yet.
- When we have a node that is connected to two arrows, that means to get to this node, we have two tasks needs to be done, and we always take the **maximum time** of these two tasks to calculate the **Latest Completion Time** of that node which is connected to these two tasks.

Formula:

Earliest Start time for a task = Earliest Start time for the task before plus the Duration of the task before.

ESB = ESA+DA

The explanation according to the example below:

(ES) Earliest Start time for node 2 = Earliest start time for node 1 + duration of task A.

ES for node 2 = ES for node 1 + D for task A

Note: D is the Duration

In case we have two arrows connected to the node we are trying to calculate its earliest start time we do the above formula on both options, then we choose the maximum time, and put it in the ES box for that node.

Look at the example below:

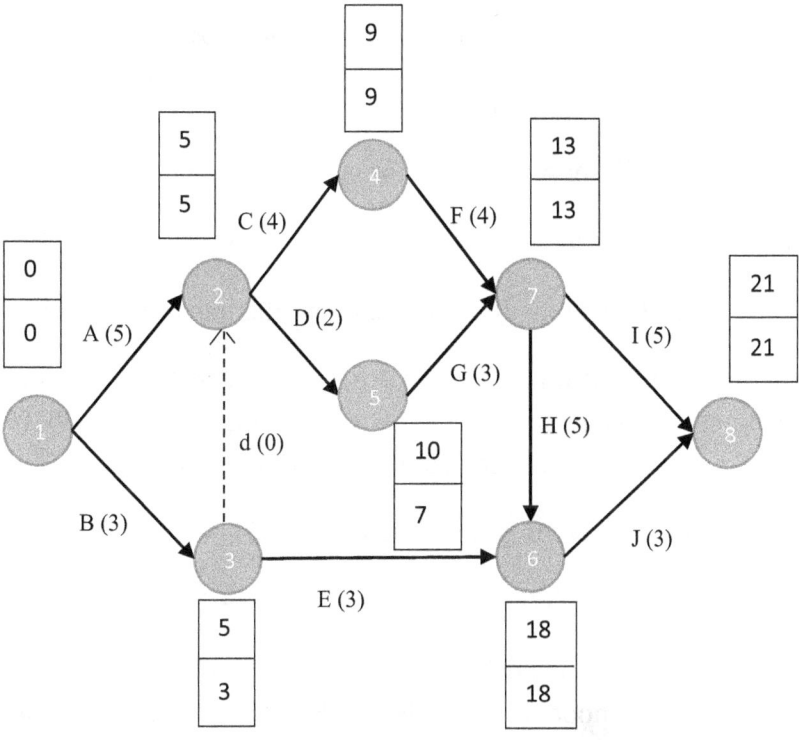

If we want to calculate the earliest start time for node 7 for example, we should calculate the two options 4 and 5 and use the maximum answer of the two options to put it in the earliest start time box of node 7

The duration of task F is 4 days.

The duration of task G is 3 days.

(ES) Earliest Start time for node 7 = Earliest start time for node 4 which is the predecessor node for node 7+ duration of task F which is the task that is connected to two nodes 7 & 4.

ES for node 7 = ES for node 4 + D for task f.

We do the same for the other node and task connected to node 7.

In this example, the answer is

ES for node 7 = ES for node 4 + D for task f.

ES for node 7 =   9   +   4   = 13

Now we calculate the other option and chose the maximum result

(ES) Earliest Start time for node 7 = Earliest start time for node 5 which is the predecessor node for node 7+ duration of the task G which is the task that is connected to two nodes 7 & 5.

ES for node 7 = ES for node 5 + D for task G.

ES for node 7 =   7   +   3   = 10

The first result is 13 and 13 > 10 the second result, so we put 13 in the ES box of node 7 which is the Maximum result of both options.

Back to our example:

We have a project; the following table shows the task and their sequence and the duration of each task by days.

We need to construct the project network and find out the duration of that project and find out the critical path for the project.

Task	Predecessors	Duration (days)
A	—	5
B	—	3
C	A, B	4
D	A, B	2
E	B	3
F	C	4
G	D	3
H	F, G	5
I	F, G	5
J	E, H	3

As a start we construct the project network:

Task A and task B have no predecessors tasks so they both start at the same starting point (node).

Duration of task A is 5 days.

Duration of task B is 3 days.

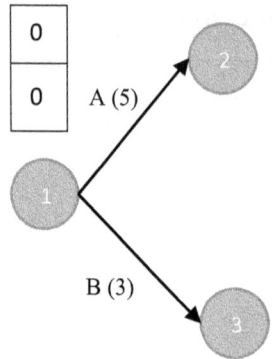

Task C:

Now task C starts where task A and task B end, and that is not possible because we cannot have two tasks start and end at the same node with different duration of time.

Duration of task A is 5 days.

Duration of task B is 3 days.

So, they can never end at the same node.

In this case, we use what we call a dummy task and we give it Zero duration

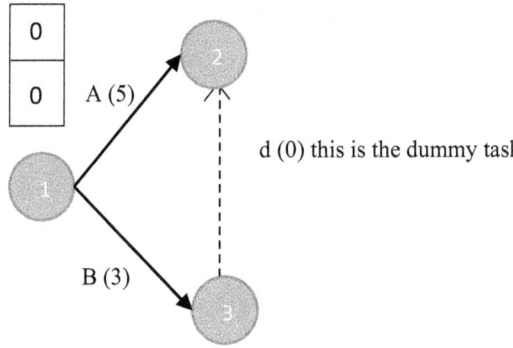

Now tasks A and B end at node 2 because the duration of task A is longer than the duration of task B so we draw a dotted arrow from B to A, now both task A and task B end at node 2.

So, task C starts from node 2 and ends at node 4. See the diagram below:

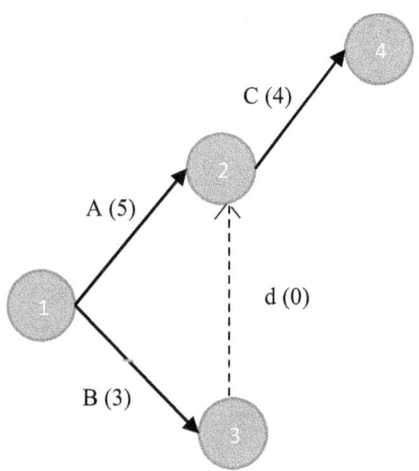

Task D:

Task D starts where task A and task B end.

See the Diagram Below:

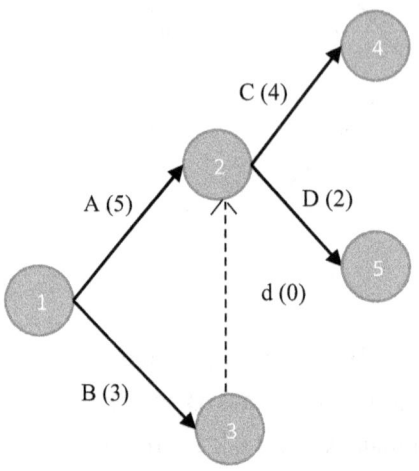

Task E:

Task E according to the table starts after its predecessor task B. Duration of task E is 3 days.

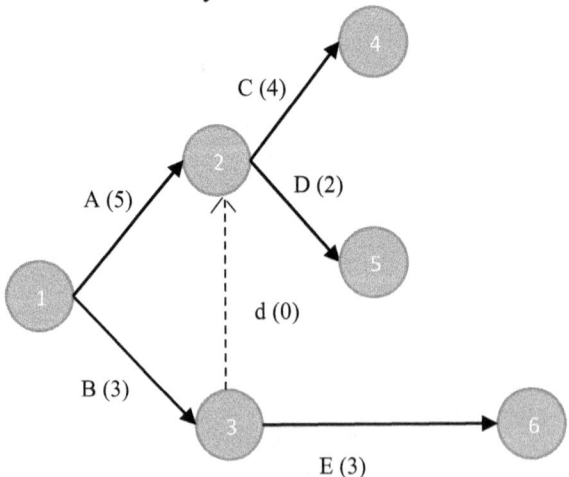

Keep going the same way till we do the whole network of the project as the following Diagram:

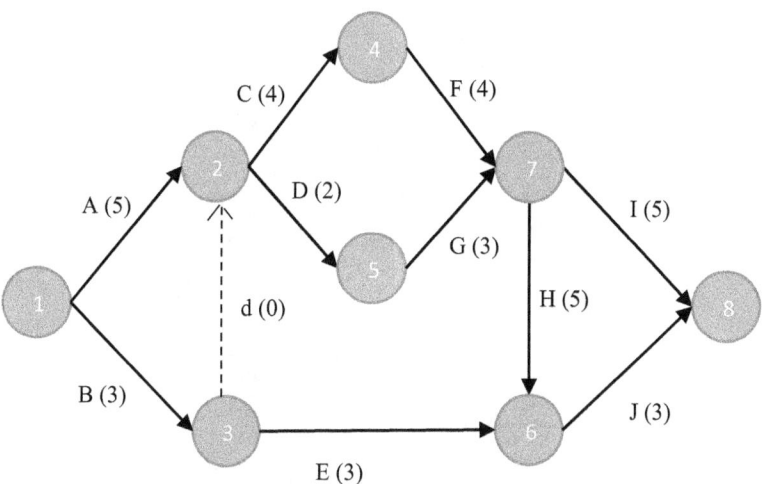

Now it is time to calculate the Latest Completion Time and the Earliest Start Time in order to get the duration and the critical path of the project.

First, we draw a rectangle divided into two boxes for each node, then we start with the Earliest Start time for each one of them until we get to the end of the project at node 8.

See the diagram on the next page:

The first Earliest start time for the first task in the project or the tasks that have no predecessors is always zero.

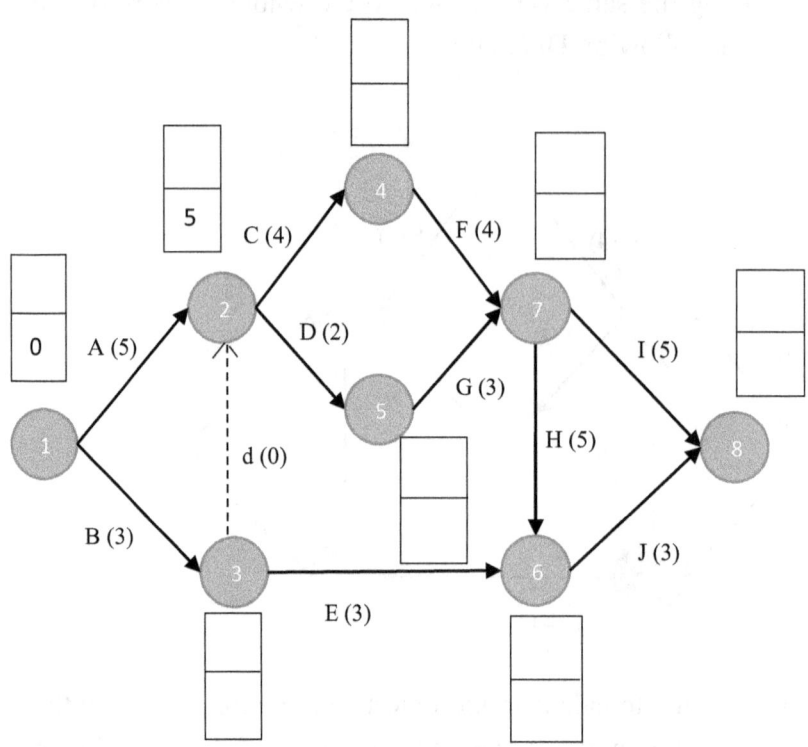

Now use the formula to calculate the ES for task C or node 2.

ESC = ESA+DA

ESC = 0 + 5 = 5

See the diagram above.

We do the same for all tasks but don't forget that whenever we have two tasks connected to the same node like node 7 in the diagram above, we use the maximum result of the two tasks connected to that node. In our case here for node 7, it is task F & task G.

(ES) Earliest Start time for node 7 = Earliest start time for node 4 which is the predecessor node for node 7+ duration of task F which is the task that is connected to two nodes 7 & 4.

ES for node 7 = ES for node 4 + D for task f.

We do the same for the other node and task connected to node 7.

In this example, the answer is

ES for node 7 = ES for node 4 + D for task f.

ES for node 7 =   9   +   4   = 13

(ES) Earliest Start time for node 7 = Earliest start time for node 5 which is the predecessor node for node 7+ duration of the task G which is the task that is connected to two nodes 7 & 5.

ES for node 7 = ES for node 5 + D for task G.

ES for node 7 =   7   +   3   = 10

First result 13 > 10 the second result, so we put 13 in the ES box of node 7 which is the Maximum result of both options.

See the diagram on the next page:

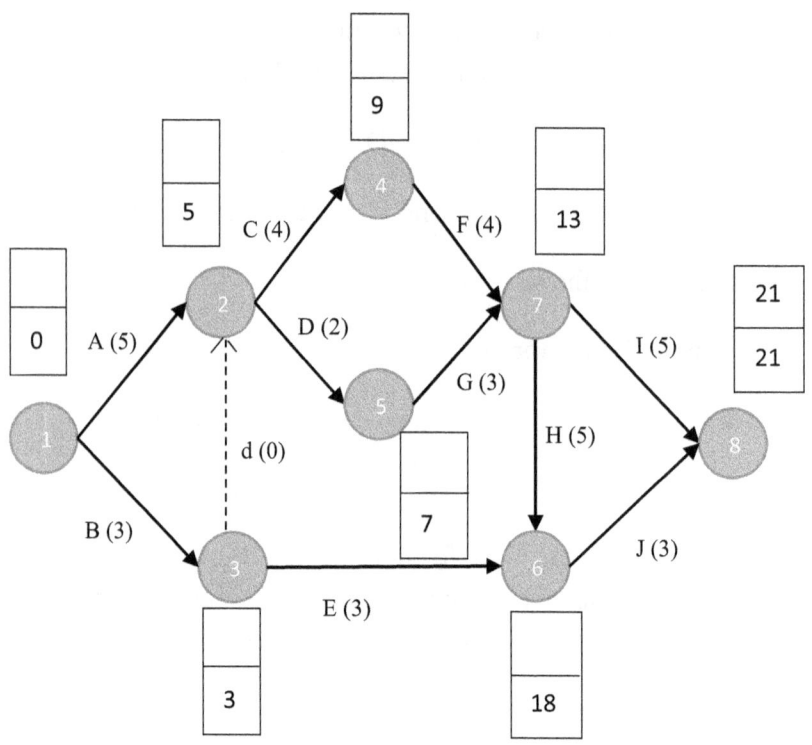

Now we have calculated all the Earliest Start Time ES for all tasks, we need to calculate the Latest completion time LC.

To calculate the Latest completion time LC we always start from the last node in the project going back to the first.

Note: The Latest completion time LC at the end of the project or the final node always equals to Earliest Start Time ES for that node because it is the duration of the project.

So, for node 8 the latest completion time is 21 = the ES of node 8. See the diagram above.

Use the following formula calculate the LC for the rest of the tasks:

LCA = LCB-DA

If you recall we learned the following rule in the LC rules:

- Going backward we start with nodes that have one arrow first then go to the nodes that have two or more arrows.

In our example here look at the diagram below the previous nodes for node 8 are none 7 and node 6 but node 6 has only one arrow so, we start with none 6.

So, the formula is:

LCJ = LCK-DJ

LCJ = 21-3 = 18

See the diagram below:

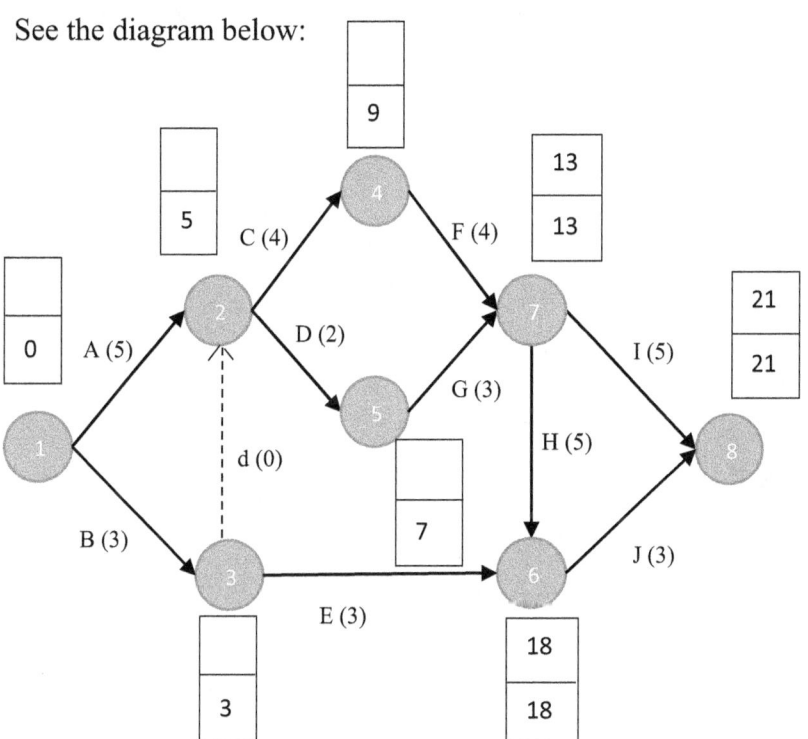

Node 7:

Now when we get to node 7 we realize that this node is connected to two tasks, so we calculate the two tasks connected to node 7 and we take the minimum result and put it in the LC box of node 7.

LCi = LCK-Di

LCi = 21 – 5 = 16 so latest completion time for task I is 16 days.

Now let's see task H which is connected to node 7

LCh = LCj-Dh

LCh = 18 – 5 = 13 now we take the **minimum result** and put it in the LC box of node 7.

13< 16 so we put 13 in the LC box of node 7 see the diagram above.

Now we continue the same way until we get the following structure.

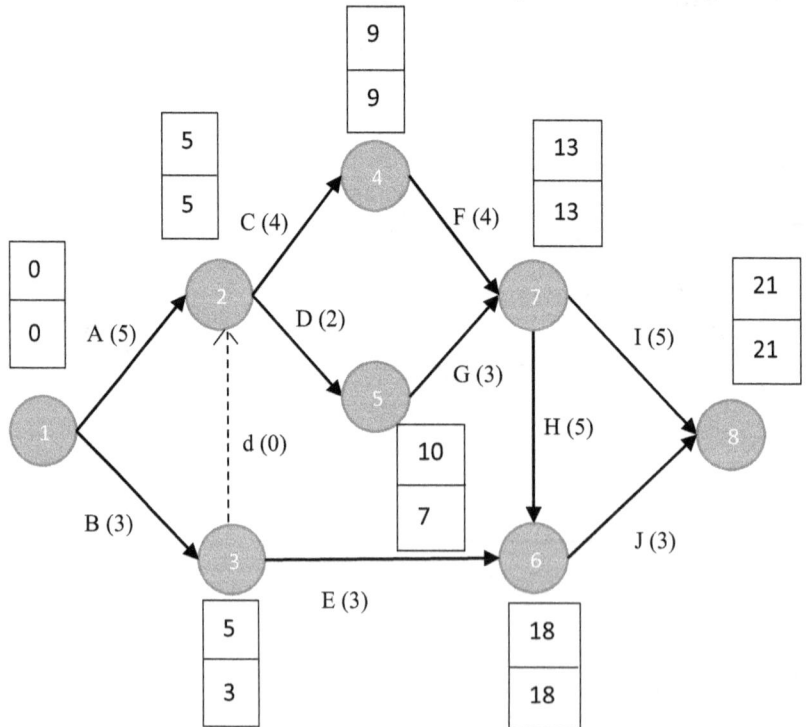

Now to find the Critical Path we highlight the arrows between the nodes that have the same numbers in both boxes of LC & ES and that will be to longest path in the project. See the diagram below:

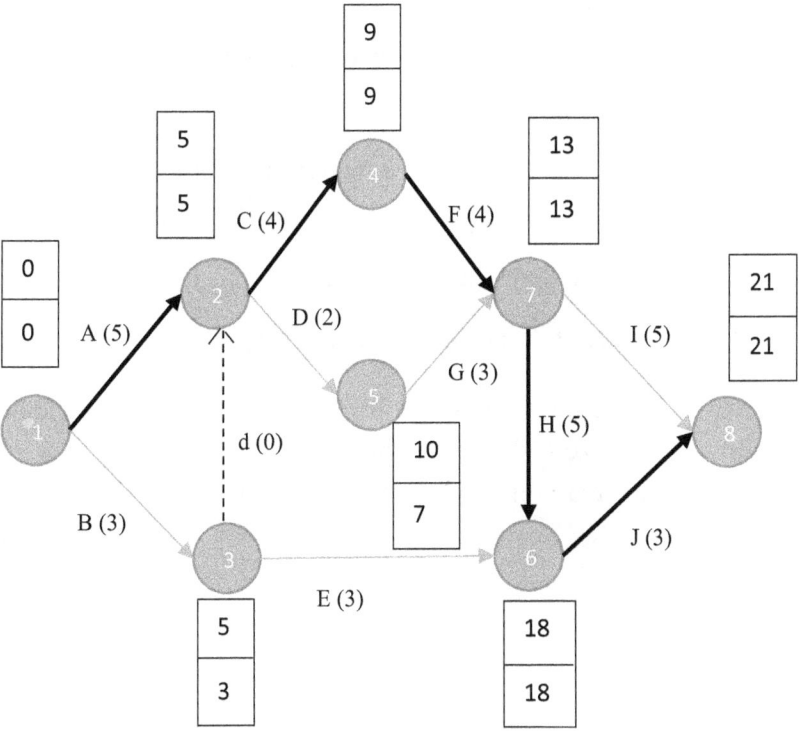

If we look at the diagram above, we find the LC and ES boxes that have the same number is:

Nodes: 1 – 2 – 4 – 7 – 6 – 8

Tasks: A – C – F – H – J

Duration: 5 + 4 + 4+ 5+ 3 = 21 so the duration of the project is 21 days

And the critical path is the path which has thick arrows in the diagram above which connects the nodes: 1 – 2 – 4 – 7 – 6 – 8 and consist of the tasks: A – C – F – H – J

After all this work we have done the following:

- Identifying all tasks needed to complete the project.
- Identifying the duration time for each task.
- Identifying the independencies or the connection among the tasks of the project.
- Determining the estimate of time duration for each task to be completed in a project.
- Determining which tasks that comprise a project, are critical in their effect on the project time to complete it.

Now management can do the needed adjustment to provide a guide to prioritize tasks and ensuring all needed resources and manpower are available for the tasks to ensure the timely project completion.

Customer Service Quality Control:

To create a customer service quality control, we can use KPI's, as we learned before, about the **Key Performance Indicator** which is an indicator that specifies the minimum acceptable amount of achievement for a certain goal.

KPI is a measure of performance within an organization, to evaluate the success of the business according to its primary objectives or strategic plan.

When we set our KPI's for the customer service quality control we can see whether we meet our KPI's or not, if not we find out the problems that don't allow us to reach our KPI's and adjust our process accordingly till we meet our desired results.

Another famous way to control customer service quality is to use the Six Sigma.

Six Sigma is a quality management theory that gives businesses the ability to **improve processes and decrease ineffective practices** by providing statistical numeric way of measurement of errors, defects, mistakes, changes, and provides corrective measures. That will reduce the errors and increase the quality of the customer service in the organization.

Financial Control

The Importance of Financial Controls:

The following are some of the most important points to know why financial control is very important to an organization:

- **Cash flow maintenance**

Financial control measures allow us to conduct the cash flow maintenance of an organization. When we have an effective financial control system, we can monitor the overall cash inflows and outflows, which results in efficient operations.

- **Resource management**

Resources are very important and essential for any organization, where controlling the resources of an organization properly will allow the management to have efficiency in the operations of that organization.

- **Profitability**

Monitoring the overall cash inflows and outflows, and having efficient operations, will increase the productivity of the organization and that comes with a direct positive effect on the profitability.

Having good financial control measures will ensure improving the profitability of any organization.

Financial Control Measures

Ratios:

Measuring the financial ratios will allow management to improve and enhance the productivity of the organization and adjust the processes accordingly to increase the profitability of the organization, and this is the main purpose of controlling.

Financial ratios are variables like cost, revenue, profit, inventory, receivables, rent, and salaries, etc.

Knowing these ratios will allow management to adjust the inputs to get the desired outputs.

Budgets:

Controlling the budget will allow department managers and project managers to know their limits so they can allocate resources accordingly, and control their expenditure to maintain cost-effectiveness along with improving productivity.

For profit-organizations we have two basic types of budget:

1- Startup budget.
2- Operational budget.

We always need to be careful about budget item categories since we should include them in our budget.

Budget can be categorized as:

- Expense budget.
- Sales budget.
- Marketing budget.
- Labor budget.

- Production budget.
- Fixed asset budget.

Cash Flow Statement

A cash flow statement is a statement that tells us how much cash is entering and leaving the organization.

In other words, a cash flow statement is a regular financial statement telling us how much cash we have on hand for a specific period.

Why do we need a cash flow statement?

- **It shows business liquidity**: we can know exactly how much operating cash flow we have in case we need to use it. So, we know what we can and what we can't afford.
- **It shows changes in assets, liabilities, and equity** in the forms of cash outflows, cash inflows, and cash being held. these three categories are considered the core of business accounting. These three categories form the accounting equation that lets us measure our performance.
- **It lets us predict future cash flows**. This is very important for making long term business plans, where we can use cash flow statements to create cash flow projections, so we can make our plans for how much liquidity our business will have in the future.

Pro Forma Statement

Companies and organizations usually submit pro forma statements when applying for most loan applications for financing and funding their businesses, when these entities need fund to develop their businesses.

This type of statement is a financial statement that shows income and expenses, or assets and liabilities that may occur in the future. Per forma statement demonstrate how additional funds will positively affect the organization's financial situation including improvement in the organization's current assets and liabilities.

Economic Value Added

The economic value added is a measure of the organization's net operating profit minus the cost of capital invested.

Economic Value Added:

(EVA) = net operating profit - cost of capital

This is an indicator of the quality of management and having positive EVA indicates good management while having negative EVA indicates poor management.

Auditing

It is always good to have even an internal or external auditing process, that will allow finding inefficiencies and allows management to find needed adjustments to processes and implement those adjustments to have the desired results.

As we see it is very important for every entrepreneur to have at least one course of accounting to learn the basics of finance in order to know how to manage his or her business properly.

Of course, each organization should have its own finance department and CFO, but it is always good for you as an entrepreneur to learn at least the basics to know how to deal with this department to lead your organization to its financial goals.

CHAPTER 16

ADJUSTING

Adjusting

Adjusting is the final step in our controlling process, it is also related to our strategic plan, after all of the endeavors that have been taken a place in your organization, adjusting is a great tool to keep the workflow on track, or at some points, you may need to change the track which means, sometimes you will find that there are some problems with the plan itself by comparing the reality to your plan, and you might find that some adjustments need to be done to the plan itself to be realistic, so not only adjusting the process or the operation.

Adjusting consist of the following three steps which are the last three steps in the controlling function:

3- Comparing actual performance with standards or goals:

After comparing the results of the actual performance with your standards you can accept or reject the outcome of the performance.

4- Analyzing deviations:

in case the standards have not been met, management should analyze why they haven't been met and try to find a solution to meet the standards. Remember that standards should be Specific, Measurable, Agreed upon, and Realistic. In this step, we also can determine whether more control is necessary or if the standard should be changed.

5- Taking corrective action:

After analyzing the deviation and determining why the standards haven't been met, management can then develop solutions for issues with meeting the standards and make changes to processes or behaviors to get the desired results.

Now after what we learned, we should recall the steps of controlling

1- Setting performance standards.
2- Measuring actual performance.
3- Comparing actual performance with standards or goals.
4- Analyzing deviations.
5- Taking corrective action.

So, the main purpose of having those measures within the controlling function is to compare actual performance with our performance standards that we have in our plan and analyze if we have any deviation, and finally take to corrective actions and adjustments according to the reports that we had during the controlling process, to meet our desired goals and fulfill the vision of our organization.

After learning the four pillars of management

Planning, Organizing, Directing, and Controlling, you are ready now as an entrepreneur to manage and lead your organization and take it to the level you are looking for.

By applying what you have learned in this book you can now create the vision, mission, and set goals for your organization or even for your life and change them into reality.

By applying the steps in this book, you will be able to change vague and fake goals and targets into reality by making them specific, measurable, agreed upon, realistic, and time-framed. In this way, you will be able to manage your goals because you have criteria to measure them and make the needed corrections to achieve the desired results.

It is like a machine that you give it ideas and it creates a mechanism for these ideas to come true by applying strategies and operational plans and then organizing the work and directing people who are responsible to do the work and controlling the process and the results and make the right corrections.

Management for Entrepreneurs

References:

Applied strategic planning
By Pfeiffer

Diagnosing and Changing Organizational Culture
By Robert E. Quinn, by Kim S. Cameron

Fundamentals of management.
By Decenzo

Business management
By IBTA

How to write a strategic plan
By Dr. Tariq Al Suwaidan & Dr. Muhammad Al Adloun